"The *Life of St Dominic* is written with a literary grace that will charm the reader, giving him at once much useful information on the state of the Church at that period and an inspiration to a higher spiritual life." *Thought*

"Father Jarrett, one of the greatest Dominican scholars today, has written a well-balanced biography . . . St Dominic is here shown as austere and kindly, flaming with enthusiasm, yet even-tempered." *Register*

"This is the standard modern biography of St Dominic, which owes not a little of its excellence to being written by one of the most outstanding Dominicans of our time."
Integrity

". . . a brief, readable account of the life and work of the founder of the Order of Preachers by one who is eminently qualified to recount the glorious tale of the Saint's career."
Review for Religious

"The *Life of St Dominic* depicts a perfect historical background as a setting for its subject and is a sound contribution to this important period of ecclesiastical history."
The Tablet

LIFE OF ST DOMINIC
(1170–1221)

BY

Bede Jarrett, O.P.

IMAGE BOOKS
A Division of Doubleday & Company, Inc.
Garden City, New York

Image Books Edition 1964
by special arrangement with The Newman Press
Image Books edition published February, 1964

NIHIL OBSTAT:
Fr. Gabriel Horn, P.P., S.T.M.
Fr. Ludovicus Nolan, O.P., S.T.M.
IMPRIMI POTEST:
Fr. Ludovicus Theissling, O.P., S.T.P. Magister Generalis.
Die 11º Februarii, 1924

NIHIL OBSTAT:
C. Schut, S.T.D. Censor deputatus
IMPRIMATUR:
Edm. Can. Surmont, Vicarius Generalis, Westmonasterii
Die 7ª Februarii, 1924

ISBN-13: 978-0-307-59097-8

Printed in the United States of America

TABLE OF CONTENTS

CHRONOLOGY

1170. Born.
1177. Leaves home for Gumiel d'Izan.
1184. Goes to Palencia University.
1189–1193. Third Crusade. Richard I.
1190. Finishes arts course and receives canonry as a theological bourse.
1194. Canon regular of Osma.
1199. Subprior.
1201. Prior.
1202–1204. Fourth Crusade. Baldwin and Dandolo.
1203. Visits the Marches on embassy with Bishop Diego of Osma.
1204. Rome.
Citeaux, Languedoc with Bishop Diego.
1205. Montpellier, Servian, Beziers, Carcassonne, Verfeuil, Fanjeaux.
1206. Montréal, Fanjeaux.
July 22. Miracle of Signadou.
November 22. Assembly of Sisters of Prouille.
December 27. Monastic life begun.
1207. Pamiers; Bishop Diego leaves, Dominic alone.
1208. January 15. Murder of Castelnau and Crusade.

1209. July 22. Sack of Beziers.

September 1. De Montfort at Fanjeaux.

1209–1211. Documents in Cartulaire (vol. i). Lives at Fanjeaux as parish priest and canon.

1211. Siege of Lavaur; Dominic and Simon.

1212. Capture of La Penne d'Ajen (July).

1213. End of February becomes Vicar General of Carcassonne; as Bishop goes to France for support for Simon.

April 22 to May 27. Prouille.

May. Reinforcements come to Fanjeaux.

June 24. Amaury de Montfort knighted at Castelnaudary in presence of Dominic.

September 12. Muret.

1214. Marriage by Dominic of Amaury de Montfort at Carcassonne in Cathedral of St Nazaire.

1215. April. Toulouse.

October. Rome.

1216. April. Leaves Rome.

July 18. Innocent III dies in Perugia.

August 28. Toulouse.

September. Leaves for Rome.

December 22. Bull of approval.

December 23. Bull of confirmation of Order.

1217. January 21. Bull about Preaching Order.

February 7. Bull placing Order under Master.

May. St Romain of Toulouse.

August 13. Prouille.

August 15. Disperses the brethren.

October. Recrudescence of heresy.

December. Milan and Bologna.

1218. January. Rome, St Sisto.

February 11. Bill recommending the Order.

June 25. Death of Simon de Montfort.

October. Bologna; Reginald sent to Bologna.

December. Prouille.

Christmas. Burgos, Segovia.

1219. February. Segovia, Madrid, Saragossa, Barcelona.

March. Toulouse and Prouille (last visit).

After Easter. Rocamadour, Orleans.

1219. June. Paris—leaves about Pentecost. Honorius driven from Rome to Viterbo.

July. Milan, Bologna.

November. Florence, Viterbo.

Christmas. Rome.

1220. February. Foundation of Nuns at St Sisto; proceeds to Viterbo; several times during this visit goes to Rome.

April. Sends St Hyacinth, etc., to North Europe.

Viterbo, Siena, Florence.

May 16. Bologna.

May 17. First General Chapter, Whit-Sunday.

May 24. Lombardy, Modena, Reggio, Parma, Piacenza, Lodi.

June 11. Milan, Bergamo, Brescia, Verona, Legnano, San Severino, Reggio, Padua.

July 22. Ronzano, Viterbo.

August 15. Bologna.

November. Imola, Faenza, Forli.

December. Rome.

1221. May. Bologna (Second General Chapter), Viterbo, Bolsena, Orvieto, Siena, Florence, Pisa.

June. Venice.

July. Bologna.

August 6. Death at Bologna.

1233. May. Discovery of relics, second tomb. Process of Canonisation at Rome, Bologna, and Toulouse.

1234. July. Canonisation by Gregory IX at Rieti.

1265. Third tomb begun.

1605. April 25. Placed in present chapel.

LIFE OF ST DOMINIC

I

THE BOY

(1170)

In an age of great adventure, when the nations about him were still young enough to be busy creating their languages and yet old enough to begin reforming their political institutions, St Dominic founded his Order. Its spirit is truly of his times contemporary with that blossoming period of European history, and it has been upheld in large measure by the continuance of the two forces then most prominent, namely the vitality of a spoken tongue victorious over a classical and learned language, and the rise of that constitutional Christian democracy which is still advancing to its fulfilment. The new languages themselves were, indeed, hardly more than a symptom of that new Christendom which was dividing into distinct nationalities; they showed the lines of the cleavage between nation and nation, and themselves hastened to widen that cleavage still more by isolating each political group in the expression of its ideals and thus cutting off the free interchange of opinions, and finally preventing that equality and sameness of thought which is the result and danger of cosmopolitan international life—a real danger, for by it the world is robbed of richness and variety.

Especially in Spain, where St Dominic was born, were these two advancing movements powerful and early. Not, indeed, that Spanish literature is found in strength much be-

fore St Dominic's own day, for long after the political
separation of Spain from Rome the hold of Latin over its
intellectual classes continued. The pronunciation even of
Latin lingered longer in its primitive form among the alien
population of the Peninsula than it had done in its own
home. But gradually even here, out of the wrack of the
Gothic and Moorish conquest and the political and religious
troubles that ensued, the purity of Latin noticeably declined,
except in the Church, in the law, and in the royal decrees
and official records; and even in these formal documents considerable lapses from classical grammar are not infrequently
found. After these troubles had passed, three chief dialects
emerged—Galician, whence sprang Portuguese; Valencian or
Catalan, which was linked in very close resemblance with
Provençal and with the language of the Midi and of Southern France; and Castilian, which finally secured the predomi-
nance in the court and in society. Galician was the tongue
of the west, Castilian of the centre, and Catalan of the east.
This curious development of Latin was modified, as can be
guessed, by words of Arabic or Gothic origin; and, further,
under the pressure of frequent use it began to drop the
complicated formations that always beset an early language.
The more primitive the speech, the more involved and cum-
bersome are its syntax and grammar; for niceness and precision are only achieved by a very perfect use of the preposition
and of the auxiliary verb. These had light duties to perform in
the sonorous sentences of Cicero; but Spanish writers from
the tenth century onwards gave up the declension of the
noun and converted the termination of *us* into *o*. Spanish had
become a language, Roman in filiation, but more flexible,
more susceptible of shades of meaning, richer, more musical
than its parent tongue. The famous poem of the Cid, challenging the Song of Roland as the earliest and most adventurous Christian epic, is now considered to be of the twelfth
century and contemporary with St Dominic; but it is very
superior to anything of its own age, and until the thirteenth
century was nearly ended had had no fellow, for Alfonso X,
though his Galician dialect destroys the beauty and music
of his lines, was really the earliest great poet of whom history has knowledge in Spain. But before these lyrical utter-

ances came the ballads, which in Spain attained a dignity not elsewhere achieved. They were not merely the popular songs of local folklore, but were free from that comic element that is ordinarily associated even with the most tragic of them in other lands; indeed, here they rank as stately historic documents, full of national sentiment and expressing the spirit of the people in a way that was all the more astonishing because for some time yet the Peninsula was not politically unified.

At this very time, too, the Cortes, or estates general of the various kingdoms of Castile, Aragon, Navarre, and Leon, were setting an example of freedom to the other people of the West. The ideas, however, that prevailed a few years ago as to the extent of the powers of these popular assemblies have been considerably modified of late, for the claims put forward for them by Spanish writers cannot always be verified. The famous Fueros de Sobrarbe, a record of the customs of Aragon (a kingdom lying between Castile and the eastern seaboard of Catalonia), though often appealed to, has never been found, and perhaps never existed in any documentary form; yet it expressed a certain independence of spirit and idea that then marked the Spanish character. Castile lay much more under the supreme domination of the King, Aragon less so, while Catalonia gave signs which at one time seemed to portend almost a republican tendency. Yet it was in Aragon that the famous Justicia held command, who was the highest judicial officer of the country and could repeal acts even of the King himself if he considered these contrary to the fundamental laws of the kingdom. But his power was lessened in practice by the fact that for a just cause, or some considerable crime, he was himself removable by the King. This enabled the King to extort from him without much difficulty a ready and instant obedience, for he could threaten to bring accusations against him should he refuse to give way, and thus be able summarily to dismiss him.

The Cortes, or separate assemblies of clergy, nobility, and city delegates, were meeting in Aragon in 1133, and had already a real and distinct authority; in 1169 at Burgos the Cortes of Castile held their first parliament, and though the representatives of the *communidades* were summoned arbitrarily, chosen by lot or from such towns as the King might happen to select, they exercised considerable authority in correcting abuses and in the internal administration of their respective municipalities and in the matter of public morals, and this nearly a hundred years before in England the towns were ordered to send burgesses to the central parliament. The rise of Spanish literature and the growing development of Spanish commercial democracy were thus timed for the coming of Dominic.

In a passage of exceptional tenderness, Dante speaks of "happy Calaroga" (now Calaruega, a village in the province of Burgos, about twenty miles from Osma), "there where the gentle breeze whispers and wanders among the young flowers that blossom over the garden of Europe, not far from that shore where the waves break, behind which the big sun sinks at eventide." With this exquisite verse the Master Seer of mediæval visions begins to depict the saint's gentle character, an "athlete" indeed as he himself adds, yet "fair and pleasing and fragrant with holiness."

The knightly descent of St Dominic from the family of Guzman seems now generally admitted, though the evidence for it is certainly not very early. Such proofs as there are have been carefully collected and marshalled by Bremond in his *De Guzmani Stirpe Sti Dominici* (Rome, 1740), in an age when discussions of genealogies afforded interest and delight to ponderous and combative authors. The Bollandists began an attack on this tradition, but they have never answered this well-documented defence. Myths and legends have quite properly embellished St Dominic's family history with royal relationships, about which, however, the early biographers are wholly silent. Still, these natural imaginative details, such as gather everywhere round the cradles of the great, do not in any way invalidate the traditional names of his father as Felix de Guzman and his mother as Joan of Aza (beatified by Leo XII and her feast kept by the Order of Preachers on August 7). They were royal wardens of the little village, living in the tall tower still standing, the only building there of any size except the church. These had two elder children born to them, Anthony, who became a Canon of St James and vowed himself to the service of the poor and sick, and

Mannes, who eventually became not only a follower of Dominic, but a member of his Order (he was beatified by Gregory XVI and his feast is kept on July 30). A later writer, Galvanus de la Flamma,[1] speaks of a sister as well, of whom, however, we know nothing; but the statement seems to be corroborated by Gerard de Frachet (1256), who mentions in his *Vitæ Fratrum* two nephews of St Dominic "who lived in the Order in much holiness."[2]

We are told, however, by the earlier writers[3] of the mother's dream while she awaited the delivery of the child: "She thought that she bore in her womb a dog and that it broke away from her, a burning torch in its mouth, wherewith it set the world aflame."[4] This is completed by another witness, his godmother at the font, who told of her dream in which the child appeared with his forehead lit by a radiant star, the light from which made the world resplendent.[5] These visions are represented in most of the statues and pictures of the saint, and serve to distinguish him in Christian art. They complete the authentic record of his babyhood.

Of his boyhood, we know that he stayed at home till he was seven years old under his mother's care, in the little bleak village only 7,176 square yards in extent, and after that was sent off to her brother, the parish priest of Gumiel d'Izan, where again he remained for seven years. He was no doubt dispatched to the charge of his uncle because already he was marked out for the university and possibly for the priesthood. There are boys who even at that age have declared, and ultimately unfalteringly carry out, their vocation. Dominic was just such a boy, knowing perfectly his own mind and having settled his future definitely for good and all. "A clever boy," says the primitive life of him by Pedro Ferandi,[6] given to playing at being an austere monk, especially by crawling out of bed at night, "resolving rather to lie on the earth than abed," a custom to which he always clung. Again, we are told that he was little interested in games, and loved reading, so that he quickly got past the other lads who learnt Latin with him at his uncle's presbytery.[7] Just a little solemn the boy must have been, and rather sensitive or impressionable. He was always quickly moved by the sufferings of others, readily responded to the

moods of the folk about him, not at all the impassive Spaniard of popular imagination, but a delicately responsive little
person such as would naturally one day be suited to become
a great preacher. All the artistic feeling of such a calling
was his, readily compassionate, a perfect companion, joyous
always on his own account, only gloomy out of sympathy
with the gloom of others.

At fourteen he went up to the University of Palencia[8] to
take his degree in arts. Here he would have found himself
settled down to his career in the Church, for in those days,
of course, arts had to precede the study of the clerical sciences. Boys thus began either at a monastery or cathedral
school or at a university to learn the culture of their day.
Dominic had near him the Benedictine abbey of Silos and
the Premonstratensian abbey of de la Vid, but to neither
of these was he intrusted; perhaps it was his sharpness of wit
that made him chosen for Palencia, which was really a little
distance off, in the kingdom of Leon. It was not yet formally
a university, for only in 1209 was it so constituted with a
definite charter under Alfonso IX, the first Spanish university; yet always there had been in the place an air of study,
quotes Denifle,[9] where young men "might learn of wisdom
in the lap of peace." In those days wisdom began with grammar, rhetoric, and logic—a very excellent start to a boy's education, for these exercises would be either stimulants or cor-
rectives to his imaginative fancy. Rhetoric would stir his
adventurous and romantic nature and help in the training of
his memory, while grammar made him plod away at the
drudgery of lessons, and logic taught him something, at any
rate, of the laws of thought. Suppose for one moment that
you had a boy to bring up and that you intended him to
become an easy and ready talker or rather disputant, quick,
well able to choose his words, and by their means to sway his
neighbours (for such a type was the cultured product that
the Middle Ages aimed at), would you not choose to set him
down to logic, grammar, and rhetoric? After this *trivium* followed the *quadrivium*—arithmetic, geometry, music, and astronomy. It will be noticeable at once how careful the
mediæval training was to produce an accurate and scientific
temper. Almost to an exaggerated extent, as we might judge,

education centred in subjects that must have been chosen purely for their corrective force, for it was part of the tradition from Greece that had filtered through Rome to Christendom that no boy should be taught to specialise. He was to be taught just the opposite of what he was by nature, for it was considered that he had to be developed, rounded off, completed, rather than have information imparted to him. He really learnt nothing, except that he learnt how to learn everything. The mediæval child was familiar with an actual world more set on beauty than on truth; about him were raised monuments whose every twisted feature and rounded pillar and rigid shaft spoke of loveliness; grandeur and splendour shone in the streets and in the clothing of the great people; colour gleamed over all. No boy of that age could ever by nature miss the charm of art or literary achievement or the beauty of the world about; but he might easily for that reason miss the great principles of exact sciences; consequently it was to the exact sciences he was apprenticed—arithmetic, algebra, music, and astronomy.

Try to imagine the boy Dominic in such a school of discipline, the compassionate nature, the ready sympathy fortified and corrected by the accuracy of mind now demanded of him. Music always appealed to him, his voice and ear combining to express the harmonies of his thought; long years after one of the witnesses at his process of canonisation told of his gay-hearted singing, chanting as he walked "the *Ave Maris Stella* or the *Veni Creator*." Music then alone for the moment gave an outlet to his natural disposition; but the six years thus spent in mingled training, by developing his latent powers of argument and clearness of exposition and yet stimulating his artistic temperament, his adaptability to his environment, his ready understanding of another's plight or gladness, were productive of great good. They steadied and strengthened and settled him, effecting in him at the end a marvellous equanimity of character to which almost every witness at the Process alludes. It was the outstanding characteristic that all noticed, his absolute evenness of temper, whatever befell.

Then, when these six years were done, he began his theology.[10] It is to be presumed that so far he had been provided for by his family; but now as a theological student he was a candidate for the priesthood and consequently the burden of his support fell henceforth on the Bishop of his diocese; yet because at that date there were practically no funds for the support of the clerical student other than the Bishop's own revenues, the dioceses who sent their students outside the cathedral precincts or who accepted for the priesthood young men already at the university were in some difficulty to provide for their support. The usual practice, therefore, was to present them to benefices, and then out of the proceeds to pay both for the students and for their vicars who actually performed in their stead whatever priestly obligations the benefices carried with them. It is clear that this was done in St Dominic's case; he came as a boy of fourteen to Palencia; he studied arts for six years (1184–1190); then the Bishop, we are told, heard of his fame and persuaded him to join the diocese. In the process of canonisation Stephen of Lombardy[11] asserted that while a theological student at the university he was already a Canon of Osma, so that evidently Bishop Martin de Bazan, his diocesan, had appointed him to a canonry at Osma to allow him sufficient funds to carry him through his years of theological study.

Not that he needed much of this world's goods, for the few details we have of him at this time suggest a poor and a hard life. He went without wine for ten years; he left aside all the sports of his companions, chiefly, indeed, because these failed to interest him; his bed was still nothing else than the bare earth; his nights, even, were often sleepless and spent in study, and when his natural powers failed and he found his imaginative temper difficult to hold down into the narrow boundaries of theological lecturing, he turned to prayer that grace might supply what nature lacked. His only extravagance was books, though this was not for him a luxury, since they were, says his first biographer, "to him a real necessary of life."[12] The picture we have of the young man of twenty sitting up through the night to annotate his volumes is completed by the story that is told of him selling the books "covered with notes that he had made in his own handwriting" so that he might have money to give in charity, a sacrifice that few students in any age would care to make. But his own explanation of his act is as delightful as the act itself: "I could not bear to prize dead skins when living skins were starving and in want."[13] He even made attempts to sell himself that he might have money to give to others.

It seems that he was ordained priest in 1195 and returned to Osma to take up the duties of his canonry at the age of twenty-four or twenty-five.[14] Nine more years were to be spent in this retirement before he was fitted for the mission which Heaven designed for him, years in which he was to be drilled in all the discipline of the religious life, for it must be noted that the chapter of Osma had been brought to a high state of ascetic reform by Bishop Martin of Bazan, whose statutes were some time later (May 11, 1199) enthusiastically approved by Pope Innocent III.[15] These canons were grouped under the rule of St Augustine, but belonged to no order in our modern sense of the word, for it was very frequently the custom in the West for a local Bishop to endeavour to organise his household on the basis of religious life, chiefly on the lines which St Augustine had established in his see at Hippo. St Chrodegang in the eighth century had reformed the whole organisation and added a series of statutes which were intended to produce greater regularity, for these canons and the monks were confusedly intermixed. In a single monastery there might be religious living side by side who followed different rules and who changed repeatedly even the rules they were following; to obviate all these confusions, fatal to the success of religious life, measures were introduced by the Council of Mayence (813) whereby each monastery was to choose a definite rule, whether monastic or canonical, and abide wholly by its laws. Henceforward the canons became a clear and distinct body among the regular clergy. At first limited to the episcopal household, they subsequently had become independent of the Bishop and could form themselves into abbeys and priories exempt from local jurisdiction.

Between them and the monks there was this great distinction in spirit, that the canons were essentially clerics, whereas the monks were not. The canons regular specialised in the clerical sciences and developed the parochial form of life, serving from their priory or abbey the little country, or even town, parishes which were too poor to support their own priest or did not afford sufficient work to occupy a priest's week-days with full and constant labour. Hence from the ranks of the canons have come the great theologians of the Western Church, while the monks have contributed the great Scripture commentators and the great historians.

The canons of Osma were grouped, therefore, under the jurisdiction of the Bishop who had himself organised and legislated for them, and their work appears to have been to supply some of the neighbouring parishes with their clergy. But of Dominic's days here we know little more than that he seldom quitted the precincts of the cloister,[16] following an even round of life, assembling with the others in the cathedral to chant the office—"weeping for the sins of others and reading and following out the *Collationes Patrum* of Cassian," adds the primitive life of the saint.[17] We are also told that because of his "swift holiness" he was soon made subprior (1199), under the priorship of Diego d'Azevedo. When Bishop Martin died, Diego succeeded him about 1201, and Dominic became Prior and head of the chapter at the age of thirty-one.[18]

This seems, perhaps, a very gentle, even monotonous, beginning for a career that was so soon to be filled with much journeying and many adventures; but it was a crucial time for the saint in enabling him to gauge the depths of his own character and to perfect the sweetness and charm of his sanctity. In words of delicate, almost feminine refinement, Jordan of Saxony describes Dominic's life at this time—Jordan himself a man of deep and tender affection, whose still extant letters defy translation in the familiar gaiety of their style and who by sympathy was able to appreciate the attractiveness of a nature as delightful as was Dominic's. Jordan wrote his life of his hero some time before 1234, and obtained impressions of him from those others who had known the saint even in Osma: "Straightway he began to appear among his brother canons as a bright ray of sunshine, in humbleness of heart the least, in holiness the first, shedding around him the fragrance of quickening life, like the sweet scent of pine-woods in the heat of a summer's day. And advancing from strength to strength as does the wide-growing olive and the slender, lofty cypress, day and night he frequented the Church, ceaselessly devoted to prayer, scarcely venturing beyond the cloister walls, the more to find leisure for his lone thoughts with God. An especial grace had been given him by God, that of being able to sorrow for sinners, for those in trouble or in any affliction, and the thought of their misery so distressed his heart as to show itself in the outward expression of tears. His custom it was, but rarely broken, to pass the night in prayer, behind shut doors beseeching God in solemn love; and the strong cry and tears, the unspeakable groaning, which he could in no way restrain, broke out audibly from him. But there was one especial petition which he often made to God, that a true love might be his to help effectively in the saving of men's souls, deeming himself then only a real member of Christ's mystic body when he could spend his whole being on gaining men, as his Lord Jesu had spent himself for them on the Cross."[19]

Like his Master, therefore, he had first of all the long years of a patient and hidden life before the public ministry began; and considering at what age he died and how great a work he inaugurated, it is really astonishing to notice how large a proportion of his life was thus spent in solitude and peace. He did not leave the cloister till 1203, and he died in 1221. In eighteen years he established his Order, preached and laboured for the faith, and then was gathered to his rest; yet even this hardly gives a fair estimate of the compressed and intense energy of his last years. He was thirty-three years old when he left the cloister for Languedoc; he preached there for thirteen years, during which time he was too busy delivering his Gospel and disputing with heretics and following the fortunes of the crusade to devote much time or leisure to the problems which he ultimately solved. He began his Order in 1216; he ruled it for five years; then he was called to his account.

It is a standing lesson to Christian souls that the amount and endurance of their work depends far more upon the character which they have previously formed than on the years of labour that they put into life. Patiently, quietly should a man fashion and temper that sole real tool with which all that he does is finally achieved. The only thing or person on which he can always depend is himself; on himself then, above all, must he concentrate. The preacher, the organiser, the administrator, is such in virtue of his own soul; because he has learnt to control himself, he can hope to control others; because he can set in order the household of his heart, he may dream of arranging in due and precise relation the affairs and work of others; only if he has found the way to God can he dare venture to lead others in the same pathway since only he knows whither it leads. Only a man who has built carefully his character may hope one day to build the world "nearer to the heart's desire."

II

THE GREAT HERESY

(1205)

The call that broke in upon this quiet life of cloistral solitude seems strangely inharmonious with it. St Dominic was dispatched on a political embassy. As a companion to Bishop Diego he went to negotiate in 1203 a marriage between Ferdinand, the son of King Alfonso IX of Castile, and a daughter of a certain "Lord of the Marches." The contemporaries of St Dominic give no more precise details than these, of the Prince whose court the ambassadors were to visit, so that both route and destiny are unknown. However, there have been conjectures in plenty as to the ultimate goal of their journey. The probability inclines to a Northern Scandinavian kingdom, Denmark or Sweden, though there is an attractive theory that suggests the French Marches, where Hugh de Lusignan was a ruler whose power and influence would have been of immense help as an ally to the sovereign of Castile. Even the Marches of Italy have been mentioned, because on their return journey the Bishop and Dominic visited Rome. But in reality the question is of little moment, for the embassy was important rather for what happened on the way than for the matter negotiated, since it led the Bishop and his Prior through the district of Toulouse, then the seat of a powerful gnostic heresy. The very evening of their arrival at the first house in Toulouse at which they put up they came in contact with it, for their host had himself lapsed from the faith. Dominic and he discussed religion at once and vehemently. The arguments on both sides were prolonged through the night, and it was only when the morning light streamed through the windows that the penitent innkeeper found himself on his knees, reconciled to the teaching of the Church. Fortunately Dominic's knowledge of the Catalan dialect stood him in good stead here and enabled him to talk intimately to the people whom he thus met. The success of his first venture urged Dominic to take up the work more permanently, and presumably he determined now the future career to which he felt a calling, but for the moment he had to proceed northwards on his embassy, return to the Court of Castile, and again set out with a numerous retinue under the leadership of Bishop Diego to bring back the young bride to Spain. But once more the interference of an accident drew the thoughts of Dominic to the sad state of the Midi. The girl-princess died before the band of knights and clerics could reach her father's kingdom. The cavalcade was disbanded, the Bishop with his cathedral Prior taking the opportunity to pass through Rome. There Don Diego seems to have spoken to the Pope about the state of things in France, and also to have asked leave to resign his Spanish see, partly because he thought himself unfitted for the position and partly because he was caught by the fascination of the East and wanted to convert the Tartar. Neither the Moors of Spain nor the heretics of Toulouse seem to have appealed to him as being nearer and therefore having a greater claim upon his charity, but the Pope insisted that the work of his life lay at his doors. Innocent III, who then with his splendid wisdom ruled the Church, would not listen to his talk of resigning his diocese, and told the Bishop rather to bow his back for larger burdens, for fuller work, and to hasten home, where these toils awaited him. Indeed, he whose visions as a Pontiff were wider and more idealistic than those of almost any other of the long line of Peter, was the most practical also of all that line. He aimed at the dominance of East and West by the supreme lordship of the Papacy (though he willingly admitted that he claimed no feudal dominion over kings or people), and he neglected no fitting instrument that seemed to him to help on that ideal. He corrected the King of France, released from their allegiance to King John the people of England, declared himself in favour of the mystic preaching of Francis and the Crusade of Baldwin, utilised every enthusiasm, and directed every energy that could further his project, yet he never missed the smaller details that helped to ensure his success. Never, through his idealising of the crusades abroad, did he forget the crusades at home, nor for the sake of some distant missionary enterprise cease to labour for the Catholic home parishes.

Foiled thus in his attempt to go east, Bishop Diego with his little train turned westwards for home, passing first by Citeaux on the Burgundian bank of the Saône. Here once more they came in contact with the heresy of the Midi, for it was to the Abbot of Citeaux that the Pope had intrusted the organisation of the preaching bands with which he hoped to win back the southerners to orthodoxy.

In 1205, after assisting at the Easter ceremonies, Diego[1] was so impressed with the religious life of the community that he received the Cistercian habit, but immediately left Citeaux with reinforcements of preachers whom he intended to take back with him to Spain to labour there. At Montpellier, however, they met the Abbot of Citeaux and the monks, Pierre of Castelnau and Raoul of Fontefroide, who so far had had the practical direction of the preaching expeditions in Languedoc. Everywhere the monks were discouraged, despondent. The heresy was exceedingly firmly rooted, well organised, and holding all classes to it by very tangible as well as convincing motives and arguments.

The heresy[2] itself was based upon the Eastern theory that all being was divided into matter and spirit, of which matter was essentially evil and spirit essentially good. This is a very simple and persistent belief, appealing to vague, lazy minds, and it has done, perhaps, more mischief in the world than any other form of misbelief. Of course, it is a sheer dogma, of which there cannot possibly be any proof, and it is accepted by many because it saves trouble and excuses them from thinking. Hence, also, in the last century and in this, it has appealed immensely to generations which are vague and lazy in thought, and through them created theosophy and Christian Science. Fortunately, however, in our own time it has never been wholly logical, precisely because the minds that have accepted it have been too lazy and too vague to understand their principles, and thus they retain enough of the Christianity they pretend to despise to prevent them from giving way to the full evils of their system. Christianity is based on a perfect understanding of the world, truer, saner; it rests upon the incarnation of the Son of God, the marriage of matter and spirit, of the divine and human, for "the Word became Flesh." Something, then, of this sanity remains to the modern world, something of this sense of balance, some respect for material things as being veils of the Godhead.

But the Middle Ages were much more scientific in temper than our own, more interested in mathematics than we are, more philosophic, less conventional, more daring. We have already seen how education was based almost entirely upon the exact sciences. Something, then, of this love of exact science drove the heretics always to perfect honesty of judgement, so that they never shirked any consequences of their beliefs. The Catholics were equally logical and, believing in prayer, respected contemplative life as the highest activity of the soul; and, believing in God's omnipotence, saw no difficulty in miracles; and, believing God had become man, could not feel any objection to the possibility of his coming as bread. The heretics of the Midi equally had the courage of their convictions; they were that to us unknown thing, a logical and organised theosophy, and consequently taught an exaggerated and compulsory monasticism.

Matter was evil; hence every living thing was unclean; and physical life was the supreme and only misfortune. Matter was in itself evil, and therefore to prolong the existence of matter was evil and to reproduce matter was an even greater evil. The only real act of goodness was the getting rid of life. "In the married state, salvation is impossible," said one of the heretical prophets.[3] Said another, "The idea of parentage is the curse of the world." Said another, "To multiply human souls is to multiply damnation." Their gospel was to decry the sanctity and meaning of marriage and to cry up the celibate life, and this not out of any appreciation of its self-immola-

always on the floor. She certainly took every care of him she could, and as he was nearly always dead-tired when he came to her, she found little difficulty in managing to get him to do what she wanted. The witness of these women was borne out by a Cistercian monk who knew him all this time: "His frugality was so austere that except on rare occasions, and out of consideration for the brethren and others who might be at table with him, he ate nothing but bread and soup. . . . I never heard or knew of his having any other bed but the church, when a church was within reach; if there was no church near, he lay on the wooden floor, or on the ground, or on the wooden planks of the bed that had been got ready for him, after carefully removing all the bed-clothes."[12] And another witness speaks of his being at times "overcome by slumber, and lying down at the roadside to sleep."[13]

Side by side, therefore, with his external austerity, which was used as a weapon in this war of wits, there can be no doubt that the natural hardiness of his character was displayed in his life. From babyhood he had been in the habit of scrambling out of bed to lie on the floor, a trait which Dante picked out and sang of in the *Divine Comedy*, and this persisted with him to the end. He had no cell of his own as a religious, and died in the cell of another, wearing another's habit. But not only by austerity did Dominic accompany his Bishop in his missionary labours among the people of the Midi; under the direction of the Cistercian legates, they both settled down to the life of preaching. Their first effort was at Servian in 1206, where the lord of the manor protected the two leading Perfects, Baldwin and Thierry, and made of his castle the centre of the local organisation of the heresy. The two Spaniards challenged them to a dispute, and, since the people of the town turned out to listen to it, it must have been conducted in the language that was common alike to Catalonia and to all the Toulouse country. On foot the two preachers drew near the city, and their poverty at once captivated the populace, who insisted on this public tourney of doctrine. Knights, women, peasants, all attended, and were keenly interested in the new form of the Catholic offensive. For eight days this particular dispute lasted, and at its close, though no definite result was achieved as far as the disputants were concerned, the audience must have been considerably impressed, for they escorted the Bishop and Brother Dominic to the next stronghold of the heresy, namely Beziers. Here the efforts of the preachers seem to have been less successful, or at least the government of the town was so powerful and so averse that no enthusiasm among the people was allowed to be effective. After a fortnight, then, the two left for Carcassonne. Again eight days were taken up with disputations, but without any very satisfactory result. It was a war of wits, and there was no reason to expect that at first the new preachers would produce any very great effect. To-day Carcassonne has been restored to the condition of a mediæval city, fenced in by formal walls, and we can understand easily how in mediæval times it was completely at the mercy of its military governor. As also had happened at Beziers, this governor was favourable to the heresy, and the people would not have been free to express their agreement with the Catholics even if they had themselves wished to do so, yet the influence of the mediæval mob in all those public theological controversies was curiously potent in other ways, for it was able by acclamation to nominate the chairman and judges of the meeting, and certainly interjected remarks and applause; but to the judges was left the actual verdict, which was normally fair and impartial. Occasionally the people voted, probably by show of hands.

After Carcassonne, Verfeuil and Fanjeaux (soon to be the headquarters of Brother Dominic) were visited, and again the success was of the slightest.

In 1207, at Pamiers, the Count de Foix held a public disputation, challenging the two to defend the Catholic faith against his preachers. The new Bishop of Toulouse, already, as we shall see, a friend to Dominic, Foulques, was present, and Bishop Navarre of Conserans; of these two Foulques was the greater help, for he had been a troubadour in early life, and then, in 1199, with two of his sons, had become a Cistercian, his wife retiring also to a monastery. To the Provençal heretics, therefore, he appeared as an attractive figure, for both his poetic skill and his monasticism assured him of a very excellent welcome; to them this combination was irresistible. This conference, therefore, at Pamiers was most successful, several converts were made, including the famous Durando de Huesca—later the founder of a religious Order, called the Order of Poor Catholics[14]—and also Arnold de Compragna, the elected judge of the proceedings. At Montréal and Fanjeaux many times over disputations were arranged and took place, among others one at which happened the famous miracle of fire.

The custom of these public debates made each party produce its résumé of arguments on the particular points that were to be disputed, so that there was a regularly organised series of agenda prepared beforehand to be discussed at each meeting. On this particular occasion Dominic's *libellus* was put forward representing the Catholic side, and the various matters laid down for the day's controversy were fully discussed; but the three judges found themselves unable to agree, and in their difficulty suggested the ordeal by fire, not yet uncommon as a test in criminal trials, and even used at times to settle the doubtful authenticities of a relic. Thrice over the *libellus* was thrown into the flames, and thrice over it was returned unscathed, burnt on the outside, and charring somewhat, where it struck it, the beam of the fireplace in which the flame was kindled.

But miracles, however numerous or startling, seldom convince the beholder. He feels sure that there is a trick somewhere, though he knows that he is not clever enough to find out how it is done, and this miracle of Dominic's had no better success; so, the next year, worn out with the physical effort, and with the constant failure to make any real impression on the people, Bishop Diego went back to his diocese, holding out, however, the hope of being able to return later to the work of the missionary venture. But he died soon after he reached Osma, and henceforward Dominic took command of the scattered band.

Then in 1208, on January 15, occurred the assassination of the legate Peter of Castelnau which resulted in the letting loose of a crusade, adding the horrors of war and carnage to the confusion of the heretical and Catholic dispute, for the war that followed was a wild and bloody adventure, political feuds crossing and stiffening the religious quarrel, while the persistent antagonism between North and South found this a ready pretext for breaking out in redoubled fury, in which acts of terrible ferocity and of hideous treachery were perpetrated by both sides. The protagonist of the South was Raymond of Toulouse, a man of much religion and little conscience, full of devotion, but devoid of honour or truth or morality. Still, it must be remembered for him that he had his back against the wall and was fighting for the possession of his own estates. The opposing leader was Simon de Montfort the elder, a much finer example of Christian chivalry, yet not a man who could feel sympathy with anyone whose views differed from his own. Further, the situation was complicated by the dislike felt by the French king for the interference of non-French princes in the struggle. The Midi, it is true, for a long time had not formed part of the Capetian kingdom, but Philip Augustus had determined gradually to recover his authority in the South, and was anxious above all that no one else should have a chance of ousting him from these fertile provinces. Hence as a whole the political leaders in France and Spain were not hostile to the Court of Toulouse, and had no sympathy for, nor any wish to encourage, papal interference with the political lordship of the South. Eventually peace came at the end not by way of war but negotiation. By the Treaty of Paris in 1229 under St Louis of France Toulouse was guaranteed to its Count, whose daughter and sole heiress married the King's son, Alphonse, and at her husband's death her territory lapsed to the French crown.

But meanwhile, by a series of victories—1209 at Fanjeaux, 1211 at Lavaur, 1212 at La Penne d'Ajen, 1213 at Muret, always in the presence of St Dominic—de Montfort harried and held the country; "the first warred by prayer, the other by arms," says Nicholas Trivet, the English Dominican historian, writing a century later.[15] They were united certainly by friendship; "he conceived for the saint a very great affection," reports Jordan of Saxony; "they became so intimate that the Earl chose the saint to give the nuptial blessing to his son Amaury and to baptise the daughter who became Prioress of St Antoine at Paris," adds Humbert de Romans (about 1250).[16] The General Chapter of the Order in 1256 ordained that "in each convent in the margin of the martyrology, the day after the Feast of St John Baptist, should be added: *This day, in the County of Toulouse, died, worthy to be remembered, the noble Earl Simon de Montfort, zealous lover of the faith and friend of the blessed Dominic.* Let this obit be recited, that the brethren on this day may pray for him and for his race which is joined to the Order by so many ties of affection and gratitude."[17] But already Dominic had seen the need of some other way than war for securing the conversion of the heretics; neither force of arms, nor the use of the secular power in its repressive, inquisitorial form, were likely to be of final service.[18]

One evening, in the hot summer of 1206, before the Bishop had left for Osma, Dominic sat reading outside the north gates of Fanjeaux. It was the Feast of St Mary Magdalen (July 22), and his mind had turned to the story of the woman that was a sinner and had become "the Apostle of the Apostles." He sat there tired and perplexed at the want of success in his mission; below him the ground sloped away into that wide and fertile valley which was the home and the support of the southern heretics, the vast pasturelands of Lauragnais and beyond, the Toulousain, with the Black Mountain range, guarding all the rich cornlands to the north and east, standing out against the sky and just touched by the setting sun. From that high place he could have marked the citadel of Carcassonne and Castelnaudary where he was to bless de Montfort's son, fresh from the ceremony of knighthood; nearer stood up Montréal, a lump in the middle distance, breaking the due level, and holding the smaller country with its towers; and then, about, the nestling villages with their dwarfed roofs, flat and crowded as they seemed from the hill, and their humped churches that gave a centre to the cluster of houses. Prayer came instinctively to him for guidance in his work, for a mark from the Mother of God of what he should do and where he should place the centre of his apostolate. As he watched, in the fast-gathering darkness, and saw the darkened shadows lengthening and hiding the landscape and shutting down the labour of the fields and the laughter of the men and women of the valley, out of the heavens descended a globe of flame, hovering awhile, as though unsure, and then, with a trail of glory following, coming down over the forlorn church of Prouille. Dominic sat and watched, hardly able to be certain that this was no trick of dreaming tired eyesight, but a sure vision. On two successive nights, as he came to this great view, it was repeated; and after the third vision, no longer in hesitation or doubt, the blessed servant of God had made up his mind. Here was the sign from Heaven that he was asking for from the Mother of God; at Prouille with its desolate church he was evidently to begin his work, and then he would find out his way to the purpose of his life. Men spoke afterwards of that vision and marked the spot on the high hill; it is still the Signadou, the "sign of God" in the language of that place.

That was the beginning of his new career, one of the chief dates of his life, perhaps the moment of his greatest grace.

It was an age of romance. Queen Eleanor of Aquitaine had made England the centre of the new movement; and on English soil were composed the tales of Arthur and all the mystic stories of that time. On the Fanjeaux plateau, over by the north gate of the city, through the hot haze of evening and against the purple gloom of the sudden twilight, another romance had shown itself that created a whole epoch of history. On the hill of the Signadou was begun all the epoch of the Friars. As a child, visions of him had come to others always with the glow of fire; now for the first time he had seen the fire for himself.

III

THE NUNS

(1206–1220)

Already these pages will have made it clear that the heretics
of Southern France were wonderfully organised and had determined to intensify and even widen their sphere of influence. There was no power possible to them which they would
not endeavour to use in their campaigns of attack and defence; consequently in that epoch of the Middle Ages they
were not likely to neglect the enormous opportunity which
the public life of that period gave to women. In the whole of
Christendom there had been and still were instances of what
women could do and had done for the advancement of any
doctrine. East and West were full of heroic figures which for
good or ill determined considerably the fate of Christian
peoples, for the break-up of older Rome meant under the
faith the increasing enfranchisement of women until the
Reformation once more re-established in Protestant lands
the supremacy of male force. In the Church controversies,
in the earlier stories of martyrdom, in the monastic movement
and its continued revival, in the political growth of countries,
in education, in all that really moulded Christian thought,
the names of women had been conspicuous, growingly conspicuous. The family particularly, which was the social centre
of the Christian organism, had been always defended and
strengthened in each succeeding age, and it necessarily lay,

as far as training went, in its earliest stages under the influence of the mother, who, indeed, in her supreme and most perfect type, was extolled in every known art. On the mother has rested the traditionary teaching of the faith; and to this was added a new force when the monastic institutions of Antony and Pachomius welcomed women into their ranks and established definite monasteries of nuns.

Both from the point of view of the family and of the convent the power of women, even under feudalism, was surprisingly great; and it endured among Catholics, even when that institution failed; whatever the reason, whether it be due to the particular honour paid to our Lady throughout the Catholic Church or not, certainly, though often treated with brutality, women had a place in the faith which no prejudice against their sex could weaken; the place of Catherine of Alexandria and her earlier and later fellow-martyrs, or of Queens Blanche and Eleanor, or of Catherine of Siena and Joan of Arc. But in Southern France an attempt was made to organise the new paganism:[1] at Montréal the mother of Aimery, its lord, and his sister, were the real leaders in the movement, and both at Fanjeaux and at Foix we read of women who figured largely in the public disputations. In the public controversy of Pamiers, held in 1207, to which we have already referred, one of the followers of St Dominic was made so irritable by the eager interruptions of Esclarmonde, the sister of the Count de Foix, that he bade her: "Get you back to your distaff." But as a matter of fact, it was precisely at home and with the distaff in hand that the most mischief was done. The inquisitorial reports from the Toulousain of 1242 and 1245 are full of evidence that goes to show that it was the home teaching of mothers and grandmothers which was really responsible for the continuance of the heresy. Converts of years' standing testified to that fact, and stated that they owed their knowledge of the teaching of the Albigensian faith to the care of their parents. Even women confessed that they themselves had deliberately and with much circumspection insisted upon detailed knowledge of the doctrines from their children. Moreover, so as to leave no possibility of leakage from their ranks, convents of "perfect" women were established as centres of apostolic missionary enterprise and as educational refuges for the children of the poorer knights and gentry. The statements of the early biographers of St Dominic are amply borne out by the records of the Toulouse Inquisition; both the primitive life of St Dominic and subsequent authors speak of the nobles of Languedoc induced by poverty "to put their daughters among the heretics to be taught and trained,"[2] and the Toulouse records[3] speak of Na Garsen Richols received at the age of two and a half, of Saura of Villaneuve at the age of seven, of Maurina de Villesisck at Cabaret scarcely at the age of discretion; of others, too, who freely admitted being brought up early to the knowledge of the doctrines of the sect. These, either as trained missionaries or as means of communicating with other rebels across districts devoted to the Catholic cause, or as wives and mothers who had to hand on the traditions to their children, were part of the organisation of the Albigeois; and it was the knowledge of this that distressed Bishop Diego and his band.

In Dominic's vision, however, of the Signadou the Bishop found his answer. The Mother of God on the feast of the penitent woman had given the solution to the Bishop through the saint. In other ways the heretics copied the Catholics in their organisation; it was time the Catholics set themselves vigorously to copy the heretics in this. Humbert de Romans tells that in that very year of 1206, at Fanjeaux, St Dominic had frequent speech with women who had fallen from the faith, and he addressed several assemblies of them, perhaps some even of the convents of the *parfaites*. Berengaria at the process of canonisation held in Toulouse told of such a meeting, to which St Dominic explained the terrible evils of the heresy, and described the heresy and spoke of it as the child of the devil. Indeed, at this meeting and in the presence of eight others, she swears to having seen the very evil spirit itself, and gives a description which reads like an old wife's tale: "In shape of a cat with the eyes of an ox, its tongue half a foot long, its tail big like a dog's and to the length of half a yard. At his command, it raced up the bell-rope and disappeared."[4] But St Dominic was not content with sermons and visions; he wanted to wrestle with the trouble at its root. These sermons were palliatives; it was a radical remedy that he sought and had found in the Signadou.

He confided his project to Bishop Diego, who was the head of the mission; and the Bishop at once took in hand the matter. He accepted the vision seen at Fanjeaux and approached the Bishop of Toulouse, on whom the Prouille church depended, and Na Cavaers, the lady of the manor, who had the right of patronage.[5] The deed of gift has not survived, but a copy remains of the authorisation which Bishop Foulques accorded to Cavaers' gift:

"Be it known to all who read or shall read this charter or who shall hear it read, that the Lord Foulques, by the favour of God humble minister of the See of Toulouse as far as in him lies, gives and grants (with the counsel and consent of the Lord Provost of St Stephen's and at the request of the Lord Dominic of Osma, as beseems his piety and mercy) the Church of St Mary of Prouille and the adjacent land to the extent of thirty feet but without tithes or first fruits, and both parties agree (as Canon Law requires) that it is for the use of women living a religious life who have been or shall have been converted by the preachers, delegated to preach against the heretics and to expel the heresy; and the tithes and first fruits which have belonged in virtue of its parochial rights to the said Church shall henceforth be paid in full to the Church of Fanjeaux and they shall hold the said Church without any feudal due or service or suit, other than the said tithes and first fruits herein granted by the Bishop from the said church of Prouille. Given in the year of our Lord 1207, in the reign of Philip, King of France."[6]

The daughter of Na Cavaers herself subsequently lapsed, returned to the faith, and became a nun at Prouille in 1246; but St Dominic (to whom it would seem that Bishop Diego committed the whole scheme, though his approval had to be sought for its inception and though he was at first described as its founder) began by gathering together nine women (the same nine among whom was Berengaria and to whom came the appearance of the devil) and lodging them in a simple dwelling "after the fashion of a convent," in buildings hastily run up by the side of the Church. These nine were all, says the primitive life,[7] "noble girls and women," and their very names have survived: Adelaïs, Raymunda Passurine, Beren-

garia, Richarde de Barbaira, Jordana, Guglielmina de Bel-
pech, Curtolana, Claretta, and Gentiana; to these converts
were soon added Manenta and Guglielmina, both from Catholic families of Fanjeaux. The miracle of the Signadou, it will
be remembered, took place on July 22; the nine women were
collected together by November 22; and on December 27 they
had begun to carry out the monastic life in the discipline and
rule already framed for them by St Dominic. Within six
months he had conceived and carried out his fine project.

The form of life that he chose for them is itself interesting.
He seems to have already made up his mind what he required these sisters to do. Says Humbert de Romans: "He
placed these servants of Christ under the protection of wonderful observance, of strict silence and permanent enclosure.
He gave them the spinning of wool as their manual work to
occupy them in the intervals of their religious exercises. He
confided the care of their souls to the friars of his Order
established outside the enclosure, keeping for himself with
the title of Prior the spiritual administration of the convent."
The primitive life assigns the foundation of the community
to Bishop Diego,[8] and states that his return to Spain in 1207
was occasioned by his desire to collect funds for its support.
It is the Bishop, then, who appoints Dominic to the priorship
of the convent, and similarly a certain William Claret to the
post of watching over and taking care of the business side of
the venture. By the time that Bernard Gui (1261–1331)
wrote his life of St Dominic, it is simply the saint who is
mentioned as the founder;[9] and certainly it is St Dominic
who had the vision, who gathered the nuns, who directed and
was charged with their welfare, and whose name figures in all
the grants made to them.

Whether or not he gave them a definite rule is not very
clear; it would seem that so long as he was near them he
trusted to his personal influence to direct them, and to his
spiritual discretion to secure for them eventually a written
constitution. A special habit was certainly chosen for them,
a white tunic, black veil, and outer cloak of unbleached wool,
and this they retained until the later vision of our Lady to
Reginald of Orleans caused St Dominic to add to this Augus-
tinian habit the white scapular.

"Thus," says Jordan of Saxony, "the servants of Christ to this day with great signs of holiness and an incomparable purity of innocence render to their Creator the homage most pleasing to him. The life they lead in this place sanctifies them and edifies their neighbour, rejoices the angels and consoles our Lord."[10]

About four months after its foundation (April 17, 1207) Beranger, Archbishop of Narbonne, gave to "the Prioress and religious of St Mary of Prouille recently converted by the teaching and example of Dominic of Osma and his companions" the Church of St Martin of Limoux with all the tithes belonging to it, till then a dependency of the Abbey of St Hilary. Other gifts soon followed, till Prouille was the centre of a series of parishes (St Julian de Bram, our Lady of Fanjeaux, St Andrew of Fontazello), of which the presentation lay with the prior and prioress of the convent. These possessions were confirmed to the nuns by the various feudal lords, Counts Raymond of Toulouse and Raymund Roger of Foix, Earl Simon de Montfort, as well as by the Apostolic See.[11] Thus were the nuns assured of a perpetual existence.

But it is clear that St Dominic had founded not only a convent of nuns, but a priory also of his friars; he had, no doubt, quite consciously established a "double monastery," as it was called. It is true that it is very clearly stated that when Bishop Diego left for Spain in 1207, the companions of St Dominic were bound to him by no vows, yet it is equally clear that they did form with him a quite definite group. The deed, already quoted, of the Archbishop of Narbonne in April, 1207, speaks of "Dominic and his companions," and another deed of August 15, 1207, refers to "the Lord Dominic of Osma and all the brothers and sisters, present and future, dwelling at Prouille," and Jordan of Saxony says the band was organised "with the assent of the Pope."[12] To all intents and purposes, then, Prouille was a double monastery, where dwelt side by side the preachers and the nuns each with their separate establishment, yet joined in one common life. The prior had to maintain the rights of the two communities, keep their deeds and the bequests, preside over the mixed council of friars and sisters, sign all contracts for sale, and appoint jointly with the prioress all the presentations to the various benefices granted to the convent, subject, of course, to the approval of the Bishop of the diocese. Directly, the prior had control over his own religious; indirectly, he had to watch and supervise the observance of the nuns. He could correct the prioress if it seemed necessary; but he could not hold a chapter of the sisters without special permission, nor could he give dispensations already refused by the prioress.

Thus it will be seen that St Dominic established contemporaneously his Order for women and for men; neither were bound to him apparently by a distinct vow until much later, when the absolute approval of the Holy See had been already acquired; nor probably until then was there any attempt to secure a rule or constitutions. Wisely and patiently the saint was finding his way, trying one plan after another, till he had made trial of what would really better secure the purpose to be achieved and the due order of the communities which he established. All this is characteristic of him. No one saw more clearly than did he what was needed; and no one was quicker than he, once the best means were discovered, in getting the work done. He knew always what he wanted, and once he saw how this could be best achieved he set to work with intense energy and rapidity, swift judgement, and amazing vitality. But he was always rather dependent upon experience than on any abstract theories as to what would work best. In the case of the nuns and of his brethren, he waited before he established any real constitutions, till the life itself proved what he should retain and what reject, and even then he was content to abide by the judgement of others, and never forced his personal opinion on them, except once only, and curiously in that instance he had to abandon his design and revert to the suggestion the others had made. A true and determined democrat, he accepted the will of his brethren, came with no hard-and-fast rules to be absolutely followed, but waited for time to determine them, and trusted to his brethren to sanction whatever constitutions might eventually be decreed.

In any case, as a canon regular, he was perfectly familiar with the "double monastery." St Gilbert, who founded his Order of double monasteries in England, was himself a canon regular, and followed, as did St Dominic, the rule of St Augustine; and this precedent so recent (St Gilbert only died in 1189) had itself a long tradition behind it. In the very age of Pepin and Charlemagne, when the canonical form of religious life was becoming formally accepted and was increasing in power and definiteness after the reform of St Chrodegang, these double monasteries for men and women were already old, and had become sometimes already an abuse. They date, perhaps, from the time of Pachomius when first we discover religious life at all, lived distinctly in community and apart from other folk.

It would seem, then, that St Dominic in founding Prouille founded simultaneously both parts of his Order.[13] Prouille is the centre of both, when at first they were rudimentary, embryonic, with little to mark them off as yet from the other existing species of religious, only gradually developing their purpose, acquiring fitting functions, finding due expression for their capacities and powers. Of the friars we shall speak later; it is necessary here to make quite sure of what he intended his nuns to accomplish. Of this fortunately there can be little doubt, for it is repeatedly insisted upon by all the early biographies that by watching the success of the heretics St Dominic saw plainly what women could do to help on the cause. He had come in Diego's train to convert the countryside; he had watched the failure of the Cistercians, and had noted at once (at least, after the Bishop's own observations), as a very obvious cause, the pomp and circumstance that the legates displayed. In dealing with people who declared all material things to be of the devil, it was hardly conciliating to exhibit precisely material splendour; such a heresy can be expelled only by fasting and prayer, by an asceticism that was also itself, perhaps, exaggerated.

Again, it was evident no less that the heretics had a trained and cultured priesthood, trained and cultured in those very points of controversy wherein they differed from the Catholic faith, and trained, moreover, publicly to discuss the various problems sufficiently clearly and interestingly to catch the wayward attention of a wandering mob. This had somehow to be met; and the answer that he made was the Order of Preachers—that is to say, it was precisely the method of St Dominic to reproduce, better organised and better trained, the very means that his rivals had shown to be successful. For the moment, at this stage of his career, he was focussing simply on the Toulousain and the Midi. He had not yet lifted his eyes to a wider plain than that which showed itself to him under the sweeping lowlands as seen from the north gate of Fanjeaux.

In the same way as he had answered asceticism by an even more terrible austerity, and teachers of heresy by a more perfectly trained band of priests, he was now to meet the mischief done by the womenfolk of the Albigeois by his convent of nuns. The heretics had made use of women to instruct others, as catechists, as spies, as messengers, induced those who were wealthy to lend their castles as centres of propaganda, worked through titles and power and through the mothers of the poorer families to push wider and wider the circle of heretical belief. It was precisely to counteract this that Prouille was established. Hence we can easily conclude what was the purpose of the new convent. The nuns were of noble birth, presumably because St Dominic particularly wanted to begin with trained teachers of the faith; they were a group of nine who had themselves been heretics and who knew the doctrines they were to answer, and who knew no less all the various schemes and methods whereby heresy itself had so rapidly spread; as though a man who wished to answer a systematised and successful propaganda should convert some of those who knew the inner working of it and should get these very people to build up a counter-organisation. Then, lest these converts should prove unstable or should fail to understand the new faith they had embraced, he particularly chose as prioress one who had always belonged to a Catholic family, an hereditary Catholic, yet who had also lived continuously amid non-catholic surroundings.[14] Indeed, if Humbert de Romans is to be believed, it was these very nine who themselves suggested the ideal: "Servant of God," he reports them to have said,[15] "if that be the truth which you have preached to us to-day, then the spirit of error has blinded us for long; for those called by you heretics have been up to the present time our preachers. We call them Good Men; we have given our whole-hearted devotion to what they have taught us; but we remain now in cruel uncertainty. Entreat the Lord for us, servant of God, that we may learn from him the faith in which we are to live and die and attain salvation." His answer was to show them in quaint guise the master whom they were really serving, and his image of the devil remained with Berengaria to the end. The Signadou followed; and Prouille was founded. It was founded therefore precisely for three purposes: apostolic, educational, and as a refuge from hostile surroundings.

The apostolate to be exercised by the nuns does not seem to have been intended to take them outside their monastery, for every early account speaks of the inviolability of the cloister, the close and strict enclosure of the Sisters. But though they could not go out, others certainly could and did come to them. Later, long after St Dominic's death, William Claret, their procurator and prior, himself a friar preacher, left that Order to become a Cistercian and tried to persuade the Sisters to follow him, but they stoutly resisted all his efforts, and would not accept the absolute seclusion he planned for them. This apostolate, therefore, was to consist of forming themselves into a centre to which those could resort who desired to learn more about the Catholic faith, and especially whence could ascend to heaven an harmonious prayer for the gift of faith for the surrounding district; and the very Aves of these women were no less to these neo-pagans than a perpetual appeal; the poverty, chastity, obedience of Prouille shows that the Albigeois had no monopoly of asceticism; the fine-spun and delicate devotions, the toll of bell by night and day, the ordered round of life which the people of Fanjeaux could see endlessly carried out before them in the valley, were arguments manifest and daily spread to their senses.

Moreover, the convent was to be an educational establishment as well; children could be taken there as well as to the associations of Laurac, directed in favour of heresy by Blanche of Montréal, the mother of Aimery, the lord of that city. Hence it would seem that children were sent here to be educated, particularly the children of the lesser nobility, who were unable to secure at home proper teachers or to place their daughters in the houses of wealthier barons. Certainly it was for this purpose that the heretics established their convents and set apart certain of their number to take up particularly that type of work; why else at Bram (not far from

Prouille) should Na Garsen Richols be clothed in the dress of the *Parfaites* at two years and a half in 1195, or Saura at Villeneuve at the age of seven, or Guiranda, "being yet quite little," be initiated to the heresy at Castelnaudary? Finally the convent was to become a refuge whither those received to the faith might escape from uncongenial heretical surroundings and find themselves better able to be instructed in and to follow the Catholic teaching. Among the Albigeois establishments such as this were already existing; at Laurac, at Castelnaudary, at Villeneuve, not only were these religious and schools as we have already seen, but there were refuge homes for those flying from their Catholic families. Through the Inquisition of Toulouse[16] we find one Doleia in 1206, who left her husband Peter Fabre, a Catholic, escaping for safety to Villeneuve, and thence further to Castelnaudary, "to Blanche and her associates," and finally to Laurac, "to Bremissande and her associates." Here at last she took the veil after a year's probation and became a novice. It was then for such a purpose, too, that Prouille was set up, to serve as a rallying-place where those who had come out of heresy could rest till their own future grew clearer and more sure. Already for Jews such places existed all over Europe, the famous *Domus conversorum*, whither a Jew could escape from the taunts and jeers of the Ghetto and find himself among others who had passed through like tribulations as he; so that the idea was not really a new one, but was only newly used for this particular type of convert.

Later on St Dominic was led to widen the scope of this work. For the moment all his interests centred on the Midi, but gradually, especially after his visit to Rome in 1216, he became convinced that all the difficulties he was trying to overcome in the Toulousain were in a more or less degree to be encountered everywhere else; he found that he had built better than he knew, and he became practically forced into a wider scheme. Pope Innocent III had much at heart the project of uniting and reforming the scattered and relaxed religious in Rome, and had for this purpose begun to restore the convent of St Sisto, which he had confided, strangely enough, to the English Gilbertines. He died, however, before accomplishing his design, and his successor, Honorius III,

aided by Cardinal Ugolino, then took the matter in hand,
and after a certain period of indecision, eventually on December 3, 1218, asked St Dominic to take over the delicate business.[17] But at the same time, as we shall see, St Sisto, though
still belonging to the Gilbertines, was occupied by over a
hundred Dominican friars; still, the transference of the friars
elsewhere was easily arranged, for Honorius offered his family
palace of the Savelli on the Aventine to the friars, near the
ancient basilica of St Sabina, and released the Gilbertines
(of whom some religious chanced at that moment to come
to Rome to secure certain privileges and immunities from
the Pope) from their obligations, as they now found they
could not spare a sufficient number of their brethren to carry
the matter through. The convent and church of St Sabina
and the convent and church of St Sisto were both put under
St Dominic's charge. It was therefore decided, as soon as the
friars had left the place, to bring nuns to St Sisto from
Prouille and to permit any other nun in Rome who should
desire greater strictness of life to join the new community.
Eventually it was hoped that these nuns would again be sent
to the various convents of Rome, and so would effect a reform
gradually through them all. The Pope, therefore, made application "to the friars and sisters of Fanjeaux and Limoux"
(note again the "double monastery" of Prouille, a very
image of the Gilbertines to whom Pope Innocent had previously turned) to help him.

"Provided now with apostolic authority, Dominic in the
first instance addresses himself to all the nuns of Rome, but
they refuse to obey the orders of the saint or of the Pope"
—so Sister Cecilia sixty years later dictated to Sister Angelica. Sister Cecilia, at the date of which she was speaking,
was a girl of seventeen, of the family of the Cesarini,[18] and
had recently been received as a nun in St Maria in Torre in
Trastevere, near the Tiber bank, hard by the famous church
of St Cecilia. "At the convent of St Maria in Torre in Trastevere, however, containing the greatest number of all, the
saint is better received. At the head of this house is the
Venerable Sister Eugenia; she, the Abbess, and her daughters
allow themselves to be won over by the holy eloquence of
the saint and, with a single exception, promise to enter St

Sisto on one condition, namely, that with them shall go their picture of the Madonna, and that if of its own power it returns to their convent of the Tiber (as had already once happened), they shall be considered released from their obligation. To this the saint willingly agrees; in his hands the Sisters make profession anew; the blessed father now forbids them to leave the convent to visit any of their families. These, however, soon learn of this injunction, and busily hasten to the convent and reproach Abbess and Sisters alike for working the ending of so fine a house and for putting themselves under the absolute care of a mere common friar. Dominic is supernaturally sensitive to this influence and the new hostility of the Sisters, and coming one morning to say Mass at St Maria, when it is done, preaches to the Sisters, saying 'My daughters, you already regret your promise and are thinking of stepping out of the pathway of God. I want, therefore, only those who do freely decide to enter at St Sisto, to renew their profession to me once more.' Some had indeed repented of their sacrifice, but now, coming to a better mind, they all make profession anew. When this has been done the saint takes the keys of the convent and assumes authority over everything: he establishes there lay brothers who are to have charge of it day and night and who will provide the Sisters in their cloister with all they need. The Sisters are strictly forbidden to speak either to their relations or to other persons, except in the presence of witnesses."[19]

The example of this famous convent quickly spread; and in every convent of Rome there was soon a party favourable to the new reform. On the first Sunday of Lent, February 15, 1220, the buildings of St Sisto were sufficiently completed to house the Sisters of St Maria in Torre in Trastevere, some nuns from St Bibiana and other monasteries, and some ladies also who desired to follow this stricter life of contemplation. These to the number of forty-four were settled in, under the direction of the friars, and with a prioress set over them from Prouille.

The spread of this rule for convents of the Order now began in earnest. A year earlier, February, 1219, Dominic had established a monastery of his nuns in Madrid after the model of Prouille. A letter of his to them is preserved in the archives of the Order in Rome:[20] "We rejoice and thank God that he has seen fit to favour you with this holy calling and to free you from the corruptions of the world. Fight the ancient foe of the human race by means of fasting, my daughters; remember that it is only those who have fought that reach the crown. My wish is that in cloistered places—that is, in the refectory, the dormitory, the chapel, silence shall be kept; and that in every other thing the rule [of St Augustine] be duly and properly observed. Let no one leave the convent: let no one enter it—unless it be the Bishop or any other superior who may have come to preach or to make a canonical visitation. Spare yourselves neither in watching nor in the use of the discipline: obey your prioress: waste not your time in idle gossip. Since we can give you no financial aid, no endowments, you are exempt from the charge of receiving friars or any other persons. Our very dear brother, Brother Mannes, who has spared no pains to bring you to this high state, will take what steps seem to him necessary to secure its continuance, your holy and religious life. He has authority from us to make visitation of the convent, to correct what he finds amiss, and, if he so judge fitting, to change the prioress, so long as the greater number of the sisters consent thereto."

Here then, again, modelled upon Prouille, we find the same form of monasticism that we have already noted. Austerity, silence, the enclosure, obedience, poverty are all part of the same discipline. Blessed Mannes is their chaplain, but in their case the double monastery does not exist, for here there was no endowment given by the friars to the nuns; at Prouille and in St Sisto the actual monastery and its funds had been given either to the friars alone or at least to both conjointly, so that it seemed only fitting that the friars should be housed and supported out of the tithes and rights of patronage. But here there was no such determined income, so that the nuns were not obliged to accept even convert women to hospitality because of the extreme poverty of the house. Finally, just as in the case of Trastevere, St Dominic had believed wholly in the free offering of the Sisters, and would accept none but voluntary novices, so here again he laid down the principle of the election of superiors and the constitutional right of each house to choose its own. As a Spaniard, home in Spain, he could do no other.

So far, however, every allusion has been made only to the Rule of St Augustine; later a definite constitution was drawn up and submitted to Rome. Actually it came to the papal authorities directly from St Sisto, and, though really emanating from Prouille, was known in consequence as the Rule of the Sisters of St Sisto.

The nuns of Prouille were not yet officially Dominicans. They were the first fruits of the saint's harvest; they were founded simultaneously with the friars, all at first without vow or definite promise, but linked with the closer bond of affection and devotion. Still, at their beginning they were part of a wider organisation; perhaps friars as well as Sisters were members of that strange unwieldy organisation (if organisation be not too definite a word) known already as the *Tertius Ordo*, which Innocent III in a flash of brilliant administrative genius had just created.

IV

THE FOUNDING OF THE ORDER

(1206–1216)

The withdrawal of Bishop Diego[1] in 1207 left Dominic in
supreme command over the little band of workers who had
gathered round the Bishop. Officially the Abbot of Cîteaux
and the two legates, Peter of Castelnau and Raoul of Font-
froide, had jurisdiction over the whole preaching campaign,
but a good deal seems to have been left to the initiative of
St Dominic, who had a roving commission over all the country round Toulouse. His own band was evidently recruited
from various sources, some being local Catholics who were
naturally interested in the conversion of their own country,
and others being a remnant of that Spanish expedition that
had been chosen as an embassy but had become a crusade.
Yet the band was "very small," and Dominic, when the
Bishop had left, was "almost alone," his companions "as yet
for another ten years" (says the primitive life) "bound to
him by no vow of profession."[2]

At this period of his life Dominic, aged thirty-six, was beginning to realise to himself his own powers. Hitherto he
had lived his sequestered life apart from all the world. From
boyhood, partly by external accident, partly by temperament,
he had held himself aloof from those about him. Even at
Palencia he was not the kind of undergraduate who mixed
much with others, for he was a great lover of books, and was

happier reading and studying than when engaged in any other pursuit; it is, indeed, curious that one who was always described by others later in life as intensely gay and companionable, radiant with happiness and energy, should have shown in his earlier years such a solemn aspect. Was it the bleak poverty, the hard look of the level plains in all the district round Calaruega, Palencia, Osma, that bit deep into his spirit? At any rate, the consensus of opinion is unanimous as to both periods: silent and solemn as a boy, silent and solemn till he set out from Osma; then the ten years' missionary enterprise in Languedoc, then gay-hearted and restless during the last five years of life.

These ten years were then of capital importance to his character, which was developing and growing up. His boyhood, its monastic quiet, its sheltered spirit, slips from him; and as these Languedoc days pass over his head, they leave him, sure of his calling, a man of ideas and ideals, bold, original, imperial in his vision, yet to his friends the most joyous and lovable of men, without pretensions or personal ambition, thoughtful, affectionate, devout.

It is, therefore, easy to guess that these days in Languedoc which really matured him must have been strenuous in their demand on nerve and spirit. He had to face endless persecution from the heretics;[3] but his faith and sense of humour alike protected him from losing courage or from giving up his task of evangelisation. Indeed, he seems to have grown more boyish as he grew older: "Sometimes to insults were added threats of bodily harm, but these were met by him with all the greater firmness, since he actually longed for martyrdom." "Have you no fear of death?" he was asked by some astonished heretics. "What would you do if we seized you now?" "Oh," he answered with a laugh, "I would just ask you not to put me to death all at once; but gradually limb by limb, to make my martyrdom a slow one, so that hardly human in form, blinded and a mass of blood, I should have a really much finer place in Heaven." And to show that he did not know what fear was, he deliberately walked through a village which he knew was hostile to him singing loudly, so that no one could miss him; on other occasions, and in places where he was warned that his life was endangered, he several times went about openly, preached, and then, when night came on, lay down by the roadside on the village green and slept peacefully, seeming to challenge anyone to do him harm.[4] After this, he was left pretty well alone. His evident and unfailing cheerfulness probably took the interest off any persecution of him, for it was hardly worth while attacking some one who seemed all the more delighted with life on that account. By this, of course, we can see that he was the very man to take up the work of the apostolate. These solemn abbots and legates who took life very seriously never had anything like the success that Dominic had. Indeed, assassination haunted their steps. But the apostle who was always perfectly even-tempered, whom nothing ever disturbed, who kindly "thanked the man for taking him a short cut"[5] when he had been deliberately led a long way round through a stiff undergrowth of brambles, was more than any heretic could ever match. It was not as though he was flippant or unsympathetic, and he was certainly never a man whom anyone could despise. His native dignity carried him perfectly and finely through jeers and laughter and through his own sense of fun; it is Jordan of Saxony's testimony that: "Nothing disturbed the even-temperedness of his soul except his quick sympathy with every kind of suffering; and because a man's face shows whether his heart is happy or not, it was easy to see from the friendliness and joyousness of his countenance that he was perfectly at peace within. Yet in spite of his unfailing gentleness and readiness to help, no one ever could despise his radiant nature, which won over everyone who came in contact with him, and made him attract people to him from the very first."[6]

In his work, St Dominic was supported with the authority of the crusading forces, and especially by Simon de Montfort, who was much struck by the fearless character of the saint. Endowments came to him through the over-lordship which the Papal legates considered themselves free to bestow on their political representative, such as Casseneuil; and the gifts made by others were confirmed by Earl Simon in September, 1214, to "his dear brother Dominic."[7] But the feudal side of the Crusade was not of much interest to him,[8] for Dominic, to make doubly sure of these bequests and donations, applied also for their authorisation to the Counts of Toulouse and Foix. Probably as a southerner his personal feeling was in favour of the South, for the Crusade developed into a local struggle between the lords of the Midi and the northern nobility. Moreover, there were Spanish forces fighting for the Toulouse feudatories; and, after the failure of the Crusade to suppress heresy, Dominic lost all interest in the war and quietly organised his own spiritual army, which was to take the place of the defeated troops of de Montfort in the war against heresy, but not in the war against the South. His official position, however, continued still to be simply a delegate of Peter of Castelnau and the Abbot of Citeaux. The instances in which he appears to have pardoned heretics, set out in authentic documents, are such as would have come to him in that capacity, and this is expressly stated in these documents. As to the exact delimitation of these powers we know very little, but judging by analogy we presume that he had the duty of examining the various "suspects" and determining whether and to what extent they were heretical. Actually the only documents refer to his authorising the release of certain suspected persons, so that we do not know of any case in which he handed them over to the secular arm; but it is quite possible that he did do so, for he certainly was connected with the machinery that was intended to suppress heresy. But to say this is not to fall into the usual inaccuracy of writers, who consider him as the founder and inspirer of the Inquisition, an historical fallacy, wholly devoid of any vestige of truth. But it is certain that, had he been its inspirer, no one in that age, least of all the heretics, would have considered him to blame. To meet heresy with capital punishment was as much according to the opinion of that age as to meet treason with capital punishment is to ours. No heretic was burnt for the benefit of his soul or in order to force him to alter his beliefs, since, as Cromwell stated in a famous phrase (which it is to be regretted remained little more than a phrase), "the will suffereth no compulsion"; but he was put to death to prevent him spreading false doctrine about things divine.[9] No murderer is hanged to cure him of his homicidal tendency, but to discourage others from any similar designs; no seditious person is sent to prison to be there convinced of his errors, whether revolutionary or reactionary, but to prevent him from seducing others less capable of sane judgement on the affairs of government. The Church and State in the Middle Ages combined to prevent what they held to be immoral and untrue doctrine being preached to the common folk.

Even after St Dominic's death it was only with regret that the Dominican Order received the later commission of the Inquisition. Humbert de Romans as Master General (1254) ordered the friars to escape the office where they could. The provincial chapter of Cahors (1244) forbade them from accepting any money that should accrue to them through the Inquisition. The provincial chapter of Bordeaux (1257) even commanded that no friar should eat at the table of the inquisitors in any place where there was a Dominican priory. Particularly after the assassination of the inquisitors of Avignonet (May, 1242) and of St Peter of Verona (June, 1242), the Order asked to be relieved of this costly task. Innocent IV refused its petition on April 10, 1243, and the next year the Bishops of the South of France begged the Holy See to insist on retaining the services of the preaching friars. Yet the Sovereign Pontiff, at least to this extent, showed his appreciation of them by reluctantly assigning to the Franciscans the Inquisition in the Pontifical States, Apulia, Florence, Tuscany, Slavonia, and ultimately Provence. From the end of the thirteenth century till the end of the fifteenth century the Inquisition was little operative. Then in the latter epoch new conditions in Spain seemed to require its re-establishment under an Inquisitor General; and the work of re-establishment was done by Thomas Torquemada (1483–1498) and by Diego de Deza (1498–1507). These were the first and last Dominican Inquisitors General of Spain.[10]

But apart from the help that came to him from the crusading host, and especially from de Montfort, St Dominic was also blest by the friendship and guidance of his Bishop, Foulques of Toulouse. This zealous prelate, troubadour and monk, was the very best adviser whom he could have had, since the Bishop was sufficiently like him to make their views congenial, sufficiently different to make him valuable in completing the work undertaken in that district for the love of souls. Foulques had Dominic's joyous temperament, though with it he had something of the instability of the South. He continued to the end to believe in the importance of parochial organisation to meet the troubles of that time. His episcopal dignity made him devote himself to that side of church extension, and his capacity in matters of finance is amply borne out by the records of his see. Yet he saw that something more than the mere parochial system was needed both to capture and even to hold the revolted country. This need Dominic was to supply.

At the end of February, 1213, the Bishop of Carcassonne set out for France to secure reinforcements for the armies of the Crusade, and he appointed Dominic as his Vicar General during his absence. For several months the saint held this office with Stephen of Metz as his companion, and thereby acquired a knowledge of the working of a diocese, but all the same he continued his sermons, and during the period of his stay there held repeated conferences in the Cathedral of St Nazaire, in which he set out the Catholic faith, arguing and denouncing and defending. He saw steadily that by itself the parochial system was insufficient to meet the conditions of the Midi, and began to feel his way to the establishment of his Order.

As far back as 1206 he had become, under Bishop Diego, the leader of a band, which, on the Bishop's return to Spain, owned Dominic as its superior, though in nowise bound to him by any vow.[11] Prouille had made this band have a definite centre; and then on May 25, 1214,[12] came the Fanjeaux benefice and the income of Casseneuil. In July, 1215, Foulques gave this band episcopal authorisation and assigned to it one-sixth of the parochial dues, a sum of money, as it turned out, so large that the Bishop subsequently negotiated with St Dominic for its surrender to the diocese.[13] At the beginning it does not seem to have been contemplated that these preachers would remain anything more than diocesan missionaries, confined in their labours to Toulouse and, therefore, approved and succoured by the local clergy.

In that same year two companions joined St Dominic, and were the first definite recruits of whom, after William Claret, Stephen of Metz, and Dominic the Little of Spain, we have name. These two more recent adherents were both of the city of Toulouse and contributed considerably to the material advancement of the Order—Peter de Seila, like St Francis of Assisi, a rich young merchant, and Thomas on April 25, 1215. Peter gave to St Dominic "some large and rather severe-looking houses near the Castle of Narbonne where they began,"[14] so that Peter used always jestingly to say that it was he who received the Order and not the Order which received him. The jest pleased him and he loved to repeat it: all the biographers had evidently heard it, and all have carefully set it down. It became a family joke. The other, Thomas, was quite of a different stamp, rather a wonderful person altogether as it seemed to the little band. He was the intellectual recruit, a fluent preacher, learned, a thinker. This small group of preachers attracted attention under Foulques' patronage, and almost immediately began to develop into a religious community. The author of the primitive life merely mentions this community as the result of a gradual evolution; and no doubt it began to evolve from the Seila house, which first made religious life really possible to them. He notes that at once the money of Foulques, and the diocesan grant, were used to provide them with "books and other necessaries." They were scholars immediately after becoming religious, and they needed books badly, for they had begun to attend the university in the city.

St Dominic was becoming clearer now in his mind as to how he should organise an Order which was to be more mobile than the parochial system, and to complete the care of souls with a disciplined body, active, movable, independent of local resources.[15] Foulques, indeed, while accepting all this, was still thinking in terms of his diocese, but Dominic was thinking in terms of the Church. Foulques saw missionaries for the Toulousain, Dominic saw a world-wide Order. Foulques handed over to Dominic diocesan dues; but he demanded them back when he discovered that Dominic had taken his measurements for a work considerably beyond the scope of the Midi. The justice of the Bishop's claim was evident and the diocesan dues were renounced; and by so doing Dominic gave his measured judgement on the inadequacy of the mere parochial system alone and began to puzzle the Canonists by talking about a religious Order coterminous with Christendom and even larger.

In 1215, the same year, memorable for the sudden beginnings of the Friars Preachers, the third Council of the Lateran met, and Foulques attended with Dominic as his canon theologian, for Dominic was still a canon, wore his canonical habit, had privileges of precedence, and was greeted with a title in the Church. His first act was to visit Innocent III and secure approval for the Prouille foundation. This was granted on October 8;[16] the nuns were placed under the rule of St Augustine, allowed freedom of election and profession, and exempted from every authority except that of the local Bishop of Toulouse. It would seem, moreover, that St Dominic spoke at some length to the Pope on the work he was actually accomplishing, for the tenth Canon of the Council enacted this new regulation: "Amongst the means for best securing the salvation of Christian souls, the most necessary is the bread of the Sacred Scriptures. Yet it happens that on account of their excessive duties or of ill-health or old age, or the strong opposition of heresy, or even of their lack of learning—a grievous fault and intolerable in a Bishop—prelates are unable themselves (especially in large dioceses) to do all the preaching that is necessary. Hence by this canon we direct them to choose men, fit for the office of preaching, whose business it shall be, when they themselves are prevented, to visit all the diocese, to preach and edify by example the flock committed to their care. Let these preachers be adequately provided for, so that they may not be forced, by lack of the sheer necessities of life, to abandon their excellent apostolate."[17] This certainly must have been suggested to the Pope or at least strongly confirmed by the report both of Foulques and Dominic, who had to describe the purpose of the Prouille establishment to Innocent in soliciting his protection and exemption for it. It would seem, therefore, that St Dominic had every reason to suppose that his project would be welcomed both by Pope and Council. But, as a matter of fact, the saint had to wait from October till April without receiving any formal authorisation for his plan. From November 11 to the end of December, 1215, the Council sat; yet even when this was over, Dominic could get no satisfaction. Rome felt very uncertain as to the prudence of the new venture, bold and daring as it seemed, for reasons that were then very urgent and almost personal.

It is perfectly clear, then, that St Dominic definitely made his proposal. He had an interview with Innocent III, and quoted Bishop Foulques and Earl Simon as his two sponsors for orthodoxy and as witnesses to his character, and he proceeded to lay before the Pontiff his scheme; it was no less than a religious Order capable of existing anywhere and devoted to the work of preaching the truths of faith. In the eyes of the Pope both the Order and its purpose were open to objection.

First of all, it was absolutely an innovation to think of a religious Order, grouped under one head and world-wide. The Benedictine ideal had made each abbey autonomous; the canonical ideal had equally left to each monastery the right of self-determination. In both cases, however, already certain modifications had taken place; the Benedictines proper had begun to found congregations, and the reforms of Cluny and still more of Citeaux had depended for their vitality on the idea of a mother abbey controlling and unifying lesser houses. The Council of the Lateran made this system compulsory and ordered the Cistercians to teach the Benedictines how to work the scheme and to appoint one of their number to attend the Chapter General of the Black monks and to offer advice as to the methods of procedure. Among the canons, William of Champeaux at St Victor, still more St Norbert and St Gilbert, had shown the possibility of such a grouping of houses. But the only real analogies that St Dominic could find to suggest the type which he wished to produce were the military orders of the Knights of the Hospital and of the Temple. These alone had the conception of a religious community flung over the whole world, composed of various *langes* or provinces or nations, governed locally by the head of each preceptory or commandery, and finding its central administration in the Grand Master and his council of officials. But even these had their definite work only in the East, and their home missions were little else than recruiting offices and barrack centres for purposes of drill and initiation and novitiate. Moreover, these had never solicited bulls of confirmation as a whole, for, as we shall see, the Papal Chancellor of Rome, when the Holy See eventually did approve of the Preaching Friars, could find no definite form to follow, and it was only gradually and in four separate bulls that the affair was finally settled.

What made the projected Order even more impossible in the eyes of the Pope was that the Lateran Council had just forbidden the multiplication of forms of religious life. Between 1063 and 1208 twelve such Orders, or more properly congregations, of monks and canons had come into being; and the tendency of the Church faced with this disruptive example was to try to amalgamate existing communities rather than start fresh ventures. It seemed as though anyone, anywhere, might claim a vision and in virtue of it reform or reorganise some rule of monasticism. To prevent any further spread of this seemingly separatist spirit, the Council enacted: "For fear lest an exaggerated diversity of religious rules should breed confusion in the Church, we forbid anyone at all to introduce any fresh rules. Whoever, therefore, wishes to become a religious must adopt one of the rules which have already been approved of, and whoever desires to found a religious house may do so provided that he accepts the rule and the constitutions of some authorised congregation."

The actual work of preaching the truths of Christian faith proved again too bold a plan to please the cautious minds of the Roman Court, who, as we shall show, had ample cause for suspicion in their sharp experience with the Vaudois and Humiliati. But this matter will be more properly dealt with in the next chapter.

The question of the new rule, however, was eventually decided by Innocent III, who bade St Dominic return to his band of six at Toulouse and discuss with them, as the Council had commanded, which of the approved rules they should follow. The primitive life says that the choice was to be "the common choice of all."[18] So Dominic hurried back to Prouille and summoned out from Toulouse the brethren who had in his absence already increased from six to sixteen. Strangely enough, neither the primitive life nor any of the early biographers give the names of these first companions. The primitive life expressly notes that they were about sixteen in number,[19] but it is only Bernard Guy who first tries to identify them and who states Prouille to be the place of their meeting: "These are the names of those whom I have been able to discover, Brother Matthew of France, Brother Bertrand of Garrigua in Provence, Brother Peter Seila and Brother Thomas, citizens of Toulouse, Brother Mannes of Spain, brother to the saint, Brother Michael Fabra and Brother Dominic the Little, both Spaniards, Brother John of Navarre, Brother Laurence of England, Brother Stephen of Metz, Brother Oderic of Normandy, lay brother, Brother William Claret of Pamiers, Brother Peter of Madrid, Brother Gomez, and Brother Michael de Uzero."[20] Now it will be noted at once that this list as a matter of fact only supplies us with fifteen names, and omits three names which are more or less certainly of this period, Brother Vitalis, Brother Noel, Prior of Prouille, and Brother William Raymund of Toulouse. The original six are known from the primitive life and included Peter and Thomas of Toulouse, William Claret, whom Diego had left in charge of the temporal affairs of the mission, Bertrand of Garrigua, who was preaching in the Midi before Bishop Diego left for Spain,[21] and the two Spaniards who had formed part of the Bishop's original band, John of Navarre and Dominic the Little. The sixteen religious, "all in fact and in name excellent preachers,"[22] met at Prouille in the August of 1216 and began by invoking the Holy Spirit, and then unanimously chose the rule of St Augustine. The primitive life says that "almost at once the rule of St Augustine, a mighty preacher, was chosen by these preachers-to-be, though to it were added certain stricter regulations concerning food and fast, bedding and the use of linen. Also they proposed and determined to hold no possessions lest the office of preaching should be impeded by the care of temporal things, but only to receive such revenues as would provide them with the necessaries of life."[23] Humbert de Romans adds: "As the new Order which was being founded required special statutes regarding study, preaching, poverty, and other such matters, it was necessary to choose a rule which had nothing contrary to what was to be grafted on to it, and since this rule of St Augustine contained only spiritual precepts and these few in number, it was easy to add to it all that was useful for the office of preaching." The wisdom of the choice was obvious: the rule of St Augustine was the oldest, the least detailed, of the Western rules; it was written by a cleric for clerics.

Before going to Rome for a final approbation of his Order, it was necessary for St Dominic and his companions to have some fixed place of abode, where they could carry out their rule and constitutions. There was in Toulouse a vacant priory, with a chapel dedicated to St Romain, to which a hospital was attached. This the Bishop and canons agreed to give for the use of the Friars Preachers. They assembled, therefore, early in July in the chapter room of the cathedral. There were present also, besides St Dominic and his brethren, the Bishop of Toulouse and other dignitaries of the cathedral. The provost, in the name of all, made a solemn donation to "Brother Dominic, Prior and Master of the Preachers and his companions present and future" of the Church of St Romain "to possess with all its offerings in all peace and liberty," subject to certain conditions stated and already agreed to.[24]

This compact was attested by both parties in presence of due witnesses, and the Bishop and the provost affixed their seals to the document.

Into this priory of St Romain, then, St Dominic at once transferred his friars. It was very small, and built for a hospital and not for regular observance; however, the enlargements progressed rapidly, and August 28, the Feast of St Augustine, now become their father by the choice of his rule, was celebrated with great joy by the little band. On this day also the saint received the vows of Father John of Navarre, a native of the Basque country, who having come with the Bishop to Toulouse, fell under the influence of St Dominic and attached himself wholly to one who, as he said "made himself amiable to everyone, rich and poor, Jew and Gentile, and was loved by all save heretics and enemies of the Church."[25] This Father John of Navarre was the "beloved disciple" of the saint. He lived to be present at the first translation of his body by Blessed Jordan, and bore faithful witness regarding his manner of life at the process of canonisation.

Shortly after this foundation—that is, about September, 1216—St Dominic set out once more for Rome. In October, 1216, we see by the deed in which Raymond Vital gave a house and vineyard to the friars that Bertrand de Garrigua was prior of the convent of Toulouse. Several other gifts of land were made about this time, thus enabling the friars to enlarge their buildings.

In October, then, 1216, St Dominic was once more back in Rome. But meanwhile (on July 18) Innocent III had died in Perugia, and it was a new Pontiff, Honorius III, already, however, known to him at the Papal Court as Cardinal Savelli, to whom he had to report the decision of his friars. Then a delay occurred which has usually been explained by supposing that the Roman authorities were still opposed to the projected Order; but there seems no ground for this supposition, for Innocent III had ultimately approved the scheme, although it had at first startled and troubled him. It is far more probable that Honorius was delayed in his action because of the difficulty found in drawing up the formal document required by St Dominic. Already monasteries and convents had been established by pontifical decree or at least taken under the Pope's protection (as had happened to Prouille in October of the previous year), but no Order had as yet ever ventured to ask for a solemn papal approval for its form of life. The Chancellory of Rome was therefore embarrassed by the absence of precedents in the wording of such an authorisation, for it took, in all, four Bulls before the work was properly done. On December 22 the Pope addressed his first Bull[26] to "Dominic, Prior of St Romans of Toulouse, and to his brethren, of the present and future, having made profession of the regular life," and he took under his protection the priory of Toulouse, in the ancient form of words which tradition had already made familiar. In St Peter's, before the assembled Cardinals, this approbation of the Order established at the Church of St Romain at Toulouse was promulgated. Then and there the Pope, Honorius III, signed the Bull, and the signatures of the eighteen Cardinals present were also affixed. This Bull, taken back by St Dominic to Toulouse, is still preserved in the city archives.[27] In twelve articles the Pope declares his intentions regarding the new Order and the special privileges granted to it.

Briefly they are:

1. That the Order is established in perpetuity.

2. That the goods, *i.e.*, benefices, are guaranteed to it intact and inviolable—naming them—the Church of Prouille, etc.

3. No tithes may be demanded of the friars on any pretext.

4. Permission is given to admit clerks and lay brothers.

5. After profession, none may pass into another Order, even one more austere, without consent of the prior (*cf.* No. 10).

6. The right to present to the Bishop of the diocese the priest appointed to serve any parish church belonging to them. He shall be subject to the Bishop as regards spiritual things, and as to the temporals shall depend on the Order.

7. No new or unusual obligations shall be put on the friars, and in time of interdict they may celebrate Mass and say the divine office in a low voice, with closed doors—without bells.

8. For the holy oils—consecrations, ordinations—they shall apply to the Bishop of the diocese; if he refuse without reason, to another, provided he be in communion with the Holy See.

9. The right of burial is accorded in their cemetery, not only to the friars, but to others who desire it out of devotion.

10. The prior (that is here the highest superior of the Order) shall be elected by a majority of votes.

11. All immunities, liberties, and reasonable customs acquired by the Order are guaranteed to them.

12. No ecclesiastical or secular authority shall interfere with the friars in the enjoyment of their goods without canonical sanction.

Then on December 23,[28] Honorius, putting aside all conventional formularies, endeavoured to confirm the whole order: "Honorius, servant of the servants of God, to his dear son Dominic and to the brethren who have made or shall make profession of the regular life, health and apostolic benediction. Considering that the religious of your Order will be the

champions of the faith and the true lights of the world, *We
confirm your Order*, with all its lands and possessions, present and future, and we take under our care and protection the
Order itself, together with all its possessions and privileges.
Given at Rome at St Sabina, the eleventh day before the
Kalends of January, one thousand two hundred and sixteen
in the first year of our pontificate."

But the Pope with the best of intentions had omitted from
this Bull the very purpose of the Order's existence. The Bull,
indeed, confirmed the Order but was valueless to the body of
the faithful, to bishops and priests, as an authorisation of
the preaching work of the friars—a fact which rather discon-
certed the friars at Toulouse. Left without their master
amidst many difficulties, of different nationalities, with the
responsibility of the hospital, without resources, some were
tempted to abandon the enterprise. St Dominic, perhaps,
warned by the Bishop of Toulouse, sought counsel of Honorius, so that on January 21, 1217, the Pope wrote to the
friars encouraging and consoling them and pointing out
clearly that their work was to be one of preaching. He addresses them as "his very dear sons, the prior and friars of St
Romain—preachers of the country of Toulouse." Already in
1211 St Dominic had signed a document at Cahors as
"Brother Dominic, Preacher."[29] In 1215 he described himself in another as "Brother Dominic, Canon of Osma, humble
minister of the preaching";[30] and in that same year he had
asked Innocent III to authorise an Order to be called that
of "Friars Preachers."[31] Now the title is given officially to
them all. So the Pope goes on after complimenting "those
invincible athletes of Christ, armed with the shield of faith
and the helmet of salvation," on their courage, he bids them
lawfully and authoritatively "preach the divine word in season and out of season, despite every obstacle and every re-
fusal."[32] Yet even so something had still been omitted. A
fourth Bull of February 7 bound all the friars in subjection
to St Dominic and forbade anyone to leave without his permission, except only to follow a severer rule.

At last, a religious Order, in the modern sense of the word,
had been finally established and confirmed in its work and
to a separate existence, such as till that date was unknown.

Meanwhile, the friars, numbering about sixteen, built near the Church of St Romain "a cloister and cells fit for study and an adequate dormitory."[33] To these St Dominic returned in May and remained at St Romain in Toulouse till August 13, when he gathered his religious at Prouille.

Already during his sojourn in Rome he had made friends with Cardinal Ugolino, who was, as Gregory IX, to canonise him in a Bull breathing the tenderest expressions of human friendship, and with St Francis, with whom he had so much in common and with whom he also formed a very sharp contrast. He left the city of St Peter when Easter was done, having spent all Lent in incessant preaching,[34] and lecturing in the papal palace; and after crossing the Alps and the Rhône he passed through Agde and Narbonne, where he handed a letter to the Archbishop from Pope Honorius, and at Carcassonne saw Simon de Montfort. Before he met his brethren at Prouille, he could hardly have helped being impressed by the success that the heresy had obtained, in his absence and despite all his labours. The southern cities had expelled the Crusaders; Marseilles had driven out its Bishop and outraged publicly the Eucharist and the crucifix. Provence was in uproar; Cevennes and Viviers had revolted again from Earl Simon, who was driven in spite of its unsettled state to leave Toulouse in order to strike a blow at the rebels. With the Earl's forces failing and with France definitely and sullenly opposed to his political crusade, the Pope turned to his preachers and to the University of Paris to make one last attempt to restore the country to the faith. A Cardinal legate arrived and met de Montfort on the banks of the Rhône while he was besieging Viviers; but the sacred purple only proved an excellent target to the enemy bowmen, who shot at His Eminence and succeeded in killing one of his retainers. Meanwhile Toulouse rose openly in revolt and recalled Count Raymund on September 1, 1217. Thus, when Dominic called his band together, the whole work of the Crusade was already undone.

The meeting of the Friars Preachers on August 13 at Prouille was little likely to find any of them in much hopefulness; for St Dominic the case was even worse, since he had understood from a vision that the death of de Montfort was

near. In the forlorn church of Prouille, amid the wide and
hot valley of cornfields, a sense of the futility of his venture
came on him. He spoke gloomily of the future of the Toulousain and quoted "a proverb of my own country: where
kindness fails, a man must try a stick."[35] The friars, however,
renewed their vows; and then on August 15, by a dramatic
stroke, Dominic dispersed his brethren.[36] With the vision of
all that country seen through the long windows from his
preaching stool, he spoke of the dispersal he had already long
contemplated, "We must sow the seed, not hoard it,"[37] and
added, "You shall no longer live together in this house." This
came to all of them as a sudden shock. However long it had
been determined in his heart, none of the others had expected it, and the author of the primitive life notes the sudden astonishment of all that band. De Montfort needed help;
the Pope had ordered forward the preachers and the professors; the Order itself required time for due and cautious
development: "The brethren were astounded since they knew
nothing of his vision, but dared not interfere." He was evidently a man of such authority that despite the apparent
foolhardiness of his policy no one questioned its wisdom. To
Spain returned Peter of Madrid, Michael of Uzero, Dominic
of Segovia or the Little, and Suero or Gomez. To Paris were
sent Matthew of France, Mannes Guzman, his brother, Michael of Fabra, Bertrand of Garrigua, Laurence of England,
John of Navarre, and Oderic the Norman lay brother, representing almost all the "nations" into which the university
was divided.[38] These took with them the letters of confirmation of the Sovereign Pontiff, "Ad publicandum et dilatan-
dum Ordinem."[39] St Dominic exhorted them to unlimited
confidence in God, and assured them of success.[40] He wished
them to go in absolute poverty, but John of Navarre, who
was by no means in love with that virtue, desired some sort
of provision for the way. He turned a deaf ear to all assurance
even when the saint, throwing himself at his feet, wept for
this want of confidence. Finally St Dominic consented to his
taking a very small sum. At Toulouse both Peter and Thomas
were to remain; at Prouille, Prior Noel and William Claret;
to Rome would go Dominic himself and Stephen, his long-
tried and devoted companion. But four new brethren now

joined the Order, and to instruct these in their religious life the saint agreed to remain a little longer at Prouille; these four new recruits were Arnold of Toulouse, Romeo of Livia, Poncio of Samatan, and Raymund of Miramont, who was himself to succeed Foulques in the See of Toulouse.[41]

Finally quitting Prouille in December, Dominic passed through Milan and Bologna, and took up his residence in January, 1218, at Rome.

But before the brethren had separated, he told them of his personal hope and desire to take the East as his portion and to fare off to Tartary,[42] and he urged that a permanent superior in his place would give proper cohesion to the institute. This, in spite of opposition, he forced on the reluctant friars, but gave them free choice as to who would best fill the post. They chose Matthew of France and called him Abbot, "the first and last Abbot in the Order," says the primitive life grimly, with a sense of relief,[43] adding that "later the brethren thought it better to have a Master rather than an Abbot." Thus quickly they came to a sense of their vocation in Christendom, preachers and teachers needing not so much a father as a master, a scholar, a doctor of theology, a graduate of a university, someone to inspire them with a love of learning, to fire them to become "champions of the faith and the true lights of the world."

Yet nothing was to lie outside the scope of their chivalrous undertaking. Without power or name or numbers, they were to bid for the leadership of all knowledge; for Dominic was in high hope, the Pope favourable, the brethren young and ready for any adventure.

V

THE PREACHER

(1216–1221)

Preaching certainly was in itself an adventure. We have already stated that the type of preaching which the Midi forced on the Catholic missioners was the explanation of the faith, simple, homely, direct. But this statement does not suggest the immense difficulty which in that age such a task presented, for it fails to bring to the memory of most minds the whole history of development that lay behind it, and without the knowledge of this the purpose of St Dominic and his work cannot be adequately realised.

Previously to the thirteenth century, the Church had fallen into one of those periods of decline and lethargy which mark the failure of human nature to keep at the high level of a divine ideal. The lives of many of the clergy, even of those holding high positions and places of trust, were a scandal to their flock; but, by a wonder of God's grace, the scandal had the effect of awakening the people to a consciousness of their own lack of religion. Hence its ultimate result was to stir up some of the finer natures among the faithful to supply the deficiencies of their pastors. From the laity came the first movement of reform. Now the most obvious neglect in the priestly vocation of that time lay in its abandonment of the preaching office, for though Mass and the services of the Liturgy might be at least celebrated, the voice of the pulpit was completely dumb; and it was just here, it was felt, that at the time most good could be effected.

As a consequence, groups of men here and there began to take up the work of the apostolate. Under Valdez[1] of Vaudois a definite organisation sprang into existence formed for the purpose of expounding the faith and rousing the indolent spirits of Christendom. Begun with no intention of disloyalty but rather for the purpose of strengthening the hands of the Church, this eager and zealous body was warmly welcomed by the Pontiff, Alexander III. He authorised its missionary enterprise, gave it a charter of freedom for preaching, and blessed it in its work. But it was soon realised that lay folk, who had no theological training and no preparation for understanding with much clearness the Gospel that they themselves came to announce, were in very evident danger of inaccuracy of statement when they touched on the truths of faith. This false rendering of the creed, begun in ignorance, in unconscious misstatement of dogma, by a sort of tragedy of the faith, soon became defiant heresy.

At the same time as this Vaudois' band came into its strength, there grew up a still more curious organisation, named the Humiliati. This body originated in some Lombard nobles whose disloyalty to the Emperor Henry V was punished by their being taken captive across the Alps. There, in imprisonment, they were converted from the vanities of the world and formed themselves into a penitential Order, with a habit of ashen colour and a definite work of charity to the poor and sick. By leave of the Emperor they were restored to their own cities and there continued the labours which they had begun in exile. One of the practical results of their sojourn in Germany was that they learnt and brought back an improved method in the manufacture of woollen garments, which industry they now taught to the Italian poor. But in process of time the Humiliati, too, took up the same preaching office as the Vaudois, and adopted the rule of St Benedict. Unfortunately, they had had no training in the theological sciences. Working along much the same lines as the Vaudois and hampered by the same absence of clerical education, they fell into similar false doctrine and were suspected of the same defiant heretical teaching. Pope Lucius III, in 1184, finally suppressed them, taking away their licence to preach. But in spite of the papal ban they continued to exist. Then in 1207 Innocent III, who was never afraid of enthusiasm and never allowed anyone who had the desire or ability to serve the Church to lose an opportunity for so doing, with his own far-seeing vision gave a section of them permission to resume their work. He gathered them together into monasteries, ordained certain of their number to the priesthood, and left those who lived outside the monastic walls, though tonsured, to depend for their spiritual direction on those among them whom he had ordained. It is interesting to note that these external members of the Humiliati are the origin of those various Orders of Penance which eventually became known as the Third Orders. These straggling bands of lay folk, out of which Innocent created the Humiliati, drifted under the influence of now one Order and now another, until we find them definitely assuming the name of the particular Order that, in this or that locality, had charge of their spiritual welfare.

These still had permission from the charter of Innocent III to preach—to continue, that is, without papal censure, the work for which they were originally founded. But there was this limitation put to their powers, that henceforth they should in their sermons avoid those subjects that touched on the dogma of the Church, those matters that their want of clerical training made it unsafe for them to discuss. They were not to venture outside the sphere of moral exhortation.[2] The phrase which, in the legal language of that date, expressed this limited subject-matter of sermonising was that the lay folk were authorised to preach "penance." Hence it is in this very definite meaning of a determined canonical expression and not with any reference to the scriptural significance of the words that St Francis of Assisi is stated by more than one author to have preached "penance." As an unordained preacher without any prolonged study of the sacred sciences, and yet with the very deepest love of God in his heart that drove him on to announce the wonders of the saving mercy of Christ with all the energy and zeal of an apostle, he put away from his discourses any doctrinal exposition of the creed and limited himself to calling upon all to praise God, or love him, or turn away from sin to serve him.

For St Dominic the vision of what his Order was to accomplish was something utterly different. Not penance, but the very truths of the faith were to be its message and the burden of its prophecy. It was precisely the exposition of the deepest mysteries of the Kingdom of God that he meant to be the exact purpose of his own mission and that of his children. It will be remembered that in all the accounts of his preachings in Languedoc of which we have any record, it is repeatedly stated that he argued with the heretics, that he wrote books against them, that he disputed with them in public, that the story of his enterprise among the Albigeois was a confounding of their theories by a theological defence of the Catholic creed.[3] It was exactly to overset science by science that he gathered his disciples around him. Far from avoiding the subtleties of the schools, he deliberately sought them out. As soon as he was established in the house of Peter Seila in Toulouse, the first university town he had visited since his own student days at Palencia, he took his little band of six to the lectures on theology given in the schools of the city by Alexander of Stavensby,[4] an English professor of great note at the time and ever after a friend to the Dominicans when he became in later years Bishop of Coventry and Lichfield. This was done before St Dominic had obtained papal approval for his infant society or indeed had even solicited it. It helps us to understand the hesitations of Innocent III, who would not at first give any definite answer to the petition of the saint in 1215, but sent him back to Toulouse for more definite details of his organisation, wisely delaying before he ventured to confirm solemnly an Order of Preachers whose direct purpose was to do that which the past had shown to be a most dangerous occasion for defiance of the papal authority, namely, the preaching of the theological dogmas of the Church. It shows us no less the daring of St Dominic who could thus attempt to gain approval from the Holy See for a project which went counter to the experience and legislation of that age, for not merely had the preaching of theology proved in the past a fatal liberty when taken up by those zealous souls who repined at the laxity of their day, but a General Council of the Church had just forbidden the institution of a new Order at all. Here, then, was St Dominic asking for the solemn confirmation (itself never before solicited or given) of a new Order to be devoted to the exposition of the whole cycle of the truths of the faith. Yet, perhaps, the most amazing part of the whole affair was that the confirmation was actually given and given so generously. The opening words of the Bull will be remembered, and they bore to the astonished minds of that generation a very definite meaning, a break with all the past, a setting of the work of the Preaching Friars above experience, above past legislation, and the opposition of the more conservative canonists: "Considering that the religious of your Order will be the champions of the faith and the true lights of the world, we confirm your Order." Boldly the Sovereign Pontiff puts as the very reason of his approval the novelty and dangerous vocation undertaken. The work of Rome has always been best done when she has trusted her children. St Dominic was put on his honour not to fail in loyalty to the Holy See. He lived up to his knightly oath of fealty.

This origin and historic justification of the existence of the Order of Preachers can again be seen in its development both during the lifetime and after the death of St Dominic. When his little band was to be dispersed, one portion was sent to Paris, the seat of the chief intellectual force of Europe. At the head of the friars was put by the saint one Master Matthew, "a learned man ready to meet every point of doctrine," and with him were John of Navarre and Laurence of England, of whom we are definitely told that they were sent there to complete their academic course, which was as yet unfinished. A third member of this community was Michael de Fabra, who at once took charge of the studies of the group and was accorded the title of "Lecturer." A little later by a professor of Paris,[5] John of Barastre, afterwards a Dominican himself, they were given a house and a church dedicated to St Jacques, eventually to gain for the Dominicans in France, by the fame attached to its success, the name of the Jacobins, which was also to descend to that extreme body of the French Revolution that met in the precincts whence the friars had been expelled. In 1219 the number of recruits in this convent had risen to thirty, an increase of twenty-three in fifteen months. John of Navarre himself noted: "The friars established themselves there and founded a convent where they gathered together many good clerics who afterwards entered the Order of Friars Preachers. Much property and revenues were given them and everything succeeded as blessed Dominic had predicted."[6] From Paris they spread over France, settling first in the episcopal cities for a reason that will shortly be explained. But for the immediate moment, it is sufficient to notice that even at that rudimentary stage the friars began at once both to study and to lecture, to attend the university that they might learn, and to hold classes themselves that they might teach. Meanwhile, St Dominic himself had set off for Rome, after some delay at Toulouse, where as a university centre two friars were left to found the great priory that is now one of the architectural gems of the city. Here in Rome again his work of preaching ("The office for which he had been chosen by God," says one of his contemporaries) brought him before the notice of the holy Father, who continued his patronage of the Order. The ancient church of St Sisto was given him by the Pope, but at the instigation of the Pontiff it (as we have seen) was soon made over as a convent to the reformed Roman nuns. This necessitated that the friars themselves should find another home. For this purpose Honorius handed over to them the basilica of St Sabina, to which they moved in 1220, the number of the brethren having risen from six to forty; and here it is recorded by hazard, that when the friars came over from St Sisto to make room for the growing sisterhood, they brought with them "their books."[7] In Rome as in Paris they are students.

In 1218, almost as soon as he had arrived in the heart of the apostolic city, St Dominic dispatched friars to Bologna, then the greatest university in Europe, for the study of Canon Law. On his way to Rome he had passed through Bologna, and must have determined to establish there a priory as soon as it was at all possible. After Paris and Rome, Bologna—for as a teacher and a student the Friar Preacher must choose just those cities which afford him the best opportunities for learning and for lecturing. As a matter of fact, it was at Bologna that the friars had their most signal success

from the point of view of the work that St Dominic wished
them to perform. Nearly all their recruits here were taken
from the most learned members of the university, so that
complaints began to be made that the chairs of the professors
would soon be emptied, and it would be found that the friars
were the teaching body of the city. But the success was due
largely to the character of one man, Master Reginald, Dean
of St Aignan of Orleans. Till he came, says Jordan of Saxony,
"the friars suffered all the misery of extreme poverty";[8] but
his arrival among the brethren turned the tide in their favour, a flaming soul, one of those vibrant personalities that
deflect the movements they embrace. His influence on St
Dominic is unmistakable, who was introduced to him,
through the influence of "a certain Cardinal," when Reginald
was pondering on the need for public preaching by men in
the apostolic state of poverty. He was in Rome when this
vocation came on him, and when the two had met he fell
quickly in with the project of St Dominic. Scholars and
preachers both, eager, fascinating, they had strong resem-
blances. To Dominic, "fascinated by the beauty of his face
and the eloquence of his language," Reginald at once unburdened himself and spoke of his own dreams and ambi-
tions. The two found themselves in perfect agreement; and
when Reginald was freed by his own bishop from his diocesan
obligations he was received into the Order and sent to Bologna to open a new priory and to gather new recruits. Jordan
of Saxony speaks of his "burning eloquence," his "flaming
speech," his "torrent of moving words"; and we are able to be
sure that all this was no mere wordy rhetoric, for the precise
people whom he most attracted were the junior graduates
and professors, later to figure conspicuously in the history of
scholastic theology, Moneta, Paul of Venice, Gilbert of England, Roland of Cremona, Raymund of Peñafort, Walter, the
last a brilliant professor of arts in the university. Roland was
subsequently famous as a logician who loved dearly the intellectual tourneys of his day, even in old age setting out
astride a donkey to meet any challenge of debate.

It was Reginald who, in the spring of 1219, settled the
friars in San Nicolo delle Vigne, and prepared, to both un-

knowingly, the place of Dominic's death and the site of his future tomb.

From Bologna at the end of 1217 St Dominic passed to Rome, having besides Stephen, his old comrade of Albigensian days, four new novices, of whose names three show the adhesion of the Teutonic race to the Order, Otho, Henry, Albert, and Gregory.[9] His work of preaching was constant and successful; "People were glad to hear him," says a witness at the Canonisation.[10] He seems to have devoted himself even to the hermits of the city, anchorites and anchoresses,[11] but everywhere the impression of his sermons was now extraordinarily vivid on the minds of his hearers; crowds flocked to him wherever he went, and the people, so stirred by his popularity, cut pieces off his habit to keep in memory of his stay among them.[12] A later writer of the thirteenth century, but one usually well informed, speaks particularly of a course of sermons in the Church of St Mark at the foot of the Capitoline Hill.

One result, quite naturally, was a great influx of young men to the Order. Dominic seems in some especial way to have been drawn to the young, and they in consequence to him. "One day," says Theodoric of Apoldia, "that servant of Christ had received a certain Henry, a handsome German boy of noble birth and of yet nobler character. His family were furious at his joining the Order and tried to break his infatuation, as it seemed to them, for Dominic, who, however, sent him away prudently with some other young men friends of his; Henry had safely crossed the Tiber by the Via Nomentana when his kinsfolk, who evidently were expecting this move, recognised him and pursued him. The novice speedily turned to God for help, and at once the river rose furiously and forbade any crossing, even on horseback. Frightened by the sudden rising of the river, they made no further efforts to prevent his carrying out his determination, and he, all the more strengthened in it, returned with his young friends to St Sisto, finding the ford of the Tiber once more at its normal level."[13]

Later, too, he was to receive at Paris a young student, who, gazing listlessly from his window, heard a voice singing in

French down the streets a quaint refrain or catch that
haunted him:

> *Time slips by,*
> *Leaving the world its toys;*
> *Time slips by,*
> *And we do nothing, my boys.*

At first it was only the haunting lilt of the music, its gay
sweetness, that touched him all that day; then their recur-
rence seemed to him a sign that the words carried a message:
"The very next day the young man, who was rich, gave up his
possessions and entered the Order of Friars Preachers. His
name was Guerric, and he was the first Prior of the Friars of
Metz whose convent he founded."[14]

In the October of 1218 St Dominic returned to Bologna
and stayed till December, when Reginald of Orleans replaced
him and was even more successful than the saint. Then by
the Flaminian Way he went on to Toulouse and Prouille, and
finally crossed back into Spain,[15] after an absence of
fourteen years, chiefly in order to encourage Michael of Uzero
and Dominic the Little, who had failed rather badly and
had "rejoined the blessed Father in Italy." Michael was left
alone, and Dominic with his small companion (who had been
with him of old in Toulouse)[16] crossed the Pyrenees by the
Pass of Roncesvalles in the difficulties of midwinter. He got
through, however, to Burgos, where Ferdinand III and the
Queen Mother Berengaria received him officially, and finally
to Segovia on Christmas Day. Here he stayed till February,
1219, founding his priory there and gathering by his eloquence a fervent band of preachers under the leadership of
Friar Corbolan. His route would have led him by Gumiel
d'Izan and Calaruega to Madrid; here he established a priory
and a convent, over the first of which he placed an early disciple of the Toulousain, Peter of Medina, and over the second his brother Mannes. Then, by Saragossa and Barcelona,
he passed in March to Toulouse and to Prouille, which he
saw for the last time. Prior Noel had been lately drowned,
and William Claret was now appointed to the office of prior
as well as procurator, a not altogether satisfactory choice, for
Claret had a supreme love for manual work and little attrac-

tion really for the intellectual interests that fascinated the convent nuns. From Prouille Priory, St Dominic dispatched Romeo of Livia and Arnold of Toulouse to Lyons, and at the same time restored to the Archbishop of Narbonne the Church of Limoux. Thus gradually in this last visit St Dominic plainly showed how the Order had ceased any longer to be a merely diocesan institute and had enlarged its borders, till from Paris to Rome and southwards to the high plateau of Christian Spain his friars were to be about their great apostolate.

After Easter he passed through Rocamadour,[17] the quaint, and at that period, the most famous sanctuary of France, and saw the legendary sword of Roland, as it still hangs, and remembered how twelve months before he had crossed the Valley of Roncesvalles, where it had defended for the last time the culture of the faith. Thence, by way of Orleans, he drew near to Paris,[18] and had his first and only sight of that centre of the intellectual life of his own generation. There he received William of Montferrat, who had already met him at Rome in the house of Cardinal Ugolino, and Henry the Teutonic, the earliest of the friars to study the Jewish teaching and to begin that ceaseless crusade of logic against the inconsequence of the broken fortunes of Israel. Here, too, at Paris Dominic told the story of the miracle of Master Reginald, and was listened to by a young subdeacon,[19] Jordan of Saxony, who so strangely succeeded to the mastership when Dominic himself had gone. Through June and July the saint stayed in Paris, dispersing his brethren to Limoges, Rheims, Metz, Poitiers, Orleans, stimulating their studies and particularly encouraging his earlier companions, who were rather out of their element among this newer set of graduates and professors. Peter Seila, at first the mainstay of the Order, was rather frightened to find himself, a merchant, among all these intellectual recruits. He looked at their volumes of philosophy and Scripture, and contrasted his solitary copy of the Homilies of St Gregory, and felt rather abashed in consequence. So greatly did William Claret later realise all this that he turned monk and left the company of these abstract-minded folk, but Peter consulted Dominic, who replied: "Go, my son, go in all confidence. Twice a day you shall be with me

in my prayers. Do not fail me, for you will win many souls
and be of much profit." The saint's fire re-enkindled the zeal
of Peter, and the prophecy came true.[20]

Then came the news of the Pope's flight from Rome to
Viterbo in June, so that at Pentecost Dominic set out from
Paris by way of Chatillon-sur-Seine with William of Mont-
ferrat, whom he knew would be of help to him at the Papal
Court, and with Brother John, a lay brother,[21] and thence by
Milan, Bologna, and Florence to Honorius at Viterbo.[22]
After a short stay, sick and feverish though he was,[23] he
passed on to Rome, where he spent the long winter, as he
had done in 1215, 1216, 1217, and was again to do in 1220.
In May, 1220, he went back by the Cassian Way to Viterbo
and Bologna, where on May 16, the Vigil of Pentecost, he
opened the first Chapter General of all his friars.[24] Then
followed an apostolate in Lombardy, for St Dominic found
himself placed by the Pope at the head of a crusading band,
which included various religious, monks, and canons: "We
command and order you to go with the said Dominic Prior
of the Order of Friars Preachers and proclaim the Word of
God to whomsoever he judges fit, so that the light of the
truth which you preach may lead home those lost out in the
darkness."[25] But the plan seemed now as unworkable as
earlier (though in reversed rôles) in Languedoc; and in the
end Dominic and his friars remained alone to meet the
heresy. At Cremona he saw for the second time St Francis
and was so moved by the gay poverty of his friend that, on
his return to Bologna for the Assumption, he was violently
angered by the new buildings of the priory and straight from
his interviews with the Poor Man of Assisi was affronted by
the increased height of the cells, the roofs of which the procurator had raised. Dominic dismissed the workmen, and the
place lay unfinished till the death of the saint removed the
prohibition,[26] and Jordan allowed the work to be resumed.
Dominic's sense of poverty was usually tempered by his desire to encourage study. It was only here, immediately after
his long conversation with St Francis, that he seems to have
been struck by the less destitute mendicancy of his own friars.
He was never a lover of poverty except as a means to study
and to preaching; but there were times, when more than ever

he saw the danger of its abandonment by his Order in the supposed interests of learned leisure. That very next year the Pope issued a Bull on March 29 denouncing "unknown persons, falsely calling themselves Friars Preachers under pretext of announcing the Word of God and attempting to collect money to the dishonour and prejudice of the true apostles of poverty." Here was opening the great dilemma of the Dominicans: if the friars had revenues, they would not be really poor; unless they had revenues, they would have to make money out of the sacred office of preaching. No wonder Dominic himself, to the dismay of his friars, advocated the separation of the two purposes. He suggested, though he was voted down and though he loyally accepted the wish of the majority against him, that lay brethren should govern the priories and collect the moneys, and that the friars should be little more than lodgers in the priories, which would thus be wholly under lay control.[27] Businessmen would finance and direct their affairs, while only the preaching would be done by the friars. No one, however, would agree to this, and Dominic had to relinquish his project.

The last great work of the early months of 1220 was to push the Preaching Friars out to the North and East of Europe and to add thereby the Slavonic and Scandinavian people to the field of St Dominic's labour. He had gathered from every other nation followers to himself, Spaniards, French, Normans, men from the border provinces of the Pyrenees, English, Teutons, Italians; to these were now to be added that curious Slav race, heavy but musical, the docile type that yet flames out with the spirit of the revolution; and his instruments were Hyacinth and Ceslaus, nephews of the Archbishop of Gnesen.[28] Both these young priests were Canons of Cracow, from which see their uncle had just been translated to Gnesen, and they were accompanying him on his visit to Rome. Like Reginald of Orleans, who had also been a canon, they were themselves contemplating an apostolate of preaching when they came across St Dominic, and fell at once victims to his charm and fascination. With them were two lay attendants, Henry of Moravia, a Czech, and Hermann, a German. The whole party spoke to Dominic at great length on the needs of the Eastern peoples of Christendom who lay at the open mercy of Tartars and Finns, and the pressure of the pagans of the north, and whose crusading host of Teutonic knights was not a very satisfactory bulwark of defence. The saint admitted the urgency of the plea, and would willingly have dispatched some friars to the aid of the Archbishop who made formal application for them, but he was forced to refuse because of the fewness of numbers, since already he had made more foundations than he could very easily support; but he suggested as an alternative that the Archbishop should find him apostles ready to convert all the Northern and Eastern nations. It was part of the peculiar influence of St Dominic that he succeeded in stirring up the boldness and audacity of young men, and attracted them to himself by showing them the capacities with which God had endowed them. No appeal of his was ever left unanswered so long as a young man was present to hear it. At once, then, the two Poles, the Czech, and the German all volunteered and offered themselves to carry out the high adventure. Undaunted by the hugeness of the task, unfrightened, uncowed by the dangers, they were perfectly ready to face the new enterprise. All four received the habit, remained in Rome so as to be quickly prepared by Dominic for their mission, and left for their own countries in April, 1220. The German laboured chiefly round Carinthia, the early fief of the Hapsburgs, and became prior of Friesach; the Czech worked principally in Moravia and Silesia; while Ceslaus made Prague his centre and Hyacinth, the greatest of them all, after a life of intense adventure and immense and untiring missionary enterprise, founded Dominican establishments on the Vistula and in Denmark and in Russia, and even set up in Kieff, amid the tumult of a Tartar invasion, a priory of Preaching Friars.

Enough has been said to show the precise purpose St Dominic had in view when he established his Preaching Order. He meant it not to follow the old evangelisation through moral exhortation and denunciation, but rather to spend its energies on a highly cultured attempt to interpret the truths of faith in the language of contemporary thought. The exposition of doctrine, the popularising of theology, the clear explanation of the catechism, the unlocking to the multitude of those vast treasures and resources committed to the Church for the enlightenment of the faithful, was the definite message of his mission. No wonder that a writer of our own generation has spoken of the saint as "the first minister of public instruction in modern Europe," or that Newman notes that whereas St Benedict is the symbol of the retreat of learning into the desert, St Dominic is the symbol of its return.

But before closing this study of the purpose and conditions which helped towards the furthering of St Dominic's ideal, a word must be said of another circumstance which also was of some importance in making the Dominican office of teaching as well as preaching useful and even necessary in the Church. This circumstance was the crisis which at the very moment of St Dominic's appearance occurred in the diocesan schools all over Christendom, namely, the break-up of the old organisation of European education and the difficulty of getting professors for the cathedral centres.

The Council of the Lateran that met in 1172 denounced very strongly the want of due theological training provided by the Bishops in their dioceses and ordered the immediate establishment of diocesan schools for that purpose. But though the Council of 1215 repeated the decree and commented very severely on the neglect of the Bishops in setting up these divinity lectures, it provided no machinery for enabling them to carry out its injunctions. For one reason or another it was found that the provision and continuance of these theological colleges was beyond the power of many dioceses, so that even after sixty years St Thomas, when defending his religious brethren from the attacks of certain members of the Paris professorial body and justifying their right to teach theology, could remark: "On account of the dearth of teachers, not even yet have the secular clergy been able to carry out the decree of the Lateran Council, that in each cathedral city there should be professors of theology, whereas, thanks be to God, we see the religious doing more than had been suggested in the establishing of divinity schools."[29] In fact, the Bishops seem to have considered themselves dispensed from any attempt to set up their own theological chairs if they found that the Dominicans had established a priory in their cathedral cities. At Metz the friars were welcomed by the Bishop in words that show this: "Association with them would be of great value not only to the laymen by their preaching, but also to the clergy by their lectures on the sacred sciences, as it was to the lord pope who gave them their house in Rome and to many archbishops and bishops." In this last phrase, no doubt, allusion is made to their establishments in Toulouse, Lyons, Liége, Milan, Tortosa, etc. Even in Oxford we find that for some years after their arrival all the theological acts took place in the Dominican Church, and down to the Reformation each candidate for the degree of Bachelor of Divinity had to preach one sermon in the Dominican Church before he could obtain his privileges. So also the Popes, as the Bishop of Metz stated, had appointed the Dominicans to lecture on theology to their court where the title of *Lectores Curiæ* was bestowed on them. It was a position that St Thomas himself eventually held, as also did William de Moerbeke, one of the greatest Greek scholars of the Middle Ages, a Flemish Dominican who translated into Latin for the use of Aquinas the works of Aristotle. From the *Lector Curiæ* is derived the present office at the Roman Court of the Master of the Sacred Palace.

These two facts enable us to see the way in which St Dominic was led to found his Order. On the one hand he wished to set up a body of men whose obligation it should be to preach the doctrines of the Church. At the same time he must have been aware that the clergy had no opportunity themselves of following theological courses unless they were fortunate enough to be able to afford the expense of a university course. Hence the idea came home to him of sending his disciples to the universities, primarily that they might learn and ultimately that they might teach. It does not appear that St Dominic himself, at any rate at first, realised this second part of his programme. Perhaps it was borne in upon him only when he found his sons frequenting the schools. Perhaps also the enormous influx of professors and students into the Order, especially under the rule of Jordan of Saxony, the immediate successor of the saint, itself irresistibly turned the thoughts of the friars in that direction. Of this only are we certain that the realisation of this mission must have come very early in the evolution of the Order, for in the most primitive redaction of the Constitutions, dated 1228 and possibly going even further back, this text is found: "Let no priory be established without its prior and a professor." It shows the eminently scholastic nature of the Order in the intentions of its first founders, that in every convent a chair of theology should be made compulsory. Thus Jordan of Saxony notes the vocation of the Friar Preacher to be "upright living, learning, teaching";[30] John the Teutonic, another Master of the Order, boasts that he belonged to Preaching Friars "whose proper function is to teach";[31] and Humbert de Romans, yet a third Master General who had himself known Jordan, declares that the Order of Preachers "was the first Order that had taken study for the aim of its foundation," but in a happy phrase he shows exactly in what sense he means this to be understood: "Study is not the object of the Order, but is absolutely necessary for the accomplishing of the aforesaid object (namely, preaching and the saving of souls), which cannot be achieved without study."[32]

Success, therefore, now had begun to crown the long silent efforts of Dominic, nor need it be further told in detail, nor even the gracious miracles that lit his path with heaven's stars. Journeyings were a necessity of his way, and they were undertaken in the same spirit of joy as had always marked with charm his manner of serving God. The chronicles tell of his passing over Europe, reading as he strode along the roads, talking of divine things as he toiled staff in hand to his newly rising convents, and in the lightness of his heart singing hymns and antiphons. This is the picture of the saint on which, perhaps, the imagination best loves to dwell; the wide stretching roadway, the country lanes, the cobbled streets, and over them passing the figure of the Spaniard, delicate, refined, almost feminine in its perfect profile, his black-cloaked habit that showed the white woollen tunic beneath, the tonsured head, the radiant brow; we watch him striding steadfastly the highways of Christendom and filling all Europe with his song.

VI

HIS PRAYER

(1216–1221)

But St Dominic did not intend to found a mere literary club where his apostles were to reside in between their sermons and their lectures. The opening of his campaign had been sufficient to impress him with the necessity of religious life as a formative means in the achievement of the perfect Friar Preacher. The old lesson that he had learnt in his missionary days among the austere heretics, who could so justly contrast their own severity with the worldly lives of the Catholics, had been engraved deeply into his heart. But it was not really this view of the question (austerity embraced as a means of edification) that most appealed to him, for the attitude taken up by the legates after the speech of Bishop Diego was based largely upon the external effect such conduct would have on the lives of others. This was no doubt an argument of some force, but the foundations of his reverence for the monastic life were laid much deeper. It was on account of no effect on others that austerity was made by him a badge of the higher vocation, but for the more important effect that such a life was likely to have upon the apostle himself. We may not neglect the souls of others, but our first concern is with our own. Hence when St Dominic was attending to the observance of the monastic discipline he was rather considering the apostles whom he was trying to form than those who would be edified by them, looking to the need they had themselves of holiness before they could dare appeal to the mind or heart of others. The old adage "physician, heal thyself" may at times be an unfair argument, but it is none the less a valuable truth; and to Dominic it seemed that the preacher needed to be immersed in the things of the spirit before he could hope to convince and stir the hearts of others.

Now the tendency of study by itself is simply to dry up the emotional side of human nature. In literature the professor is commonly represented as the type of man who has lost all sympathy with the troubles of suffering humanity. He is pictured as so absorbed in his own pursuits (that often look rather to the past or to the abstract or to the lifeless theories of science than to present realities) as not to be able to disentangle himself from them nor to allow himself the opportunity for realising that the past is over, that life is concrete, that life is indeed alive. The intellectual side of his interests is so fascinating that it may well seem to excuse him from the trivialities of daily conduct. For him his own world of study is evidently so real, so personal, so much more pregnant with tragedy than he can find in the ordinary trammels of existence, that he imagines he has chosen the wiser and truer part, since the present is so soon to pass and the past so eternally to abide.

Yet this attitude, which we can well understand in the men of leisured culture, is altogether inexcusable in the apostle, for his whole purpose is to help others to attain to truth, goodness, and love. He must first be ablaze himself; nor can he allow himself the sole enjoyment of his fire; he may not shield a guarded flame. He has to go outside of himself, lift himself up among the tumult of existence, make his voice ring out above the noise of the machinery of life. If he preach not the gospel there is laid on the preacher an anathema, for he has failed in the purpose of his calling, has buried his talent, or perhaps squandered it in an alien service. Therefore in the eyes of St Dominic the danger, especially for the chiefest and best of his children, would be their absorption in study, in the mere interest of the preparation, in the labour of mind, so that the labour of the ministry would become repulsive to them. In order, therefore, to insist upon the apostolic spirit being kept alive, St Dominic enforced upon his preachers the law of silence, of fast, of Divine Office said chorally, of the discipline of cloister, of poverty, chastity, and obedience. It may seem a contradiction to assert that, in order to make his apostles apostolic, St Dominic first made them monks; in order to drive them into the world he drove them from it. But the explanation of this paradox is to be found in the strange law that governs human nature: you must die to live, lose your life to find it. The danger for the Dominicans was therefore to be remedied by making them drink deep of the spiritual life, for the apostle, who has his interest in mere intellectual pursuits, will find that the tendency to remain absorbed in pure abstraction is corrected by strict monastic observance. The discipline of austerity works in the direction of setting the soul afire. Not only does it induce in the soul the high and deep thoughts that entrance a man's being, but it enables these to blossom out into action. The result is not merely to give light to his nature, but to impart to it that heat which must needs set the world ablaze. A man whose constant attention is fixed on the thought of God, whose lower nature is kept subject by discipline and fast and abstaining from flesh-meat, whose voice is perpetually spent on the praises of God, whose daily round of life is knit up with the life of his community, must become interested in things outside the mere round of his religious life. The intellectual atmosphere tends to make him a recluse, the religious atmosphere tends to make him an apostle. The one drives him to fix his gaze on God, the other to announce to the world what the vision has burnt into his soul. For Dominic, therefore, religious life was a means for the personal upbuilding of the preacher, by softening and inflaming his heart.

In consequence St Dominic insisted that his children should include in their lives, not the mere study of the sacred sciences, but also the acceptance of the religious ideal of a canon of St Augustine; to the exhausting work of preaching he added the detailed cloistral duties. Determinedly and of set purpose, he made austerity a part, an essential part, of the practice of his Order.

To begin with, there was to be the full cycle of the chanted Office. Perhaps in those days to have omitted this would have been an impossibility, for the idea had not yet been suggested of religious who would say the Divine Office in private. Even the secular parish priests were supposed by the Canon Law of that time as far as possible to make the liturgical prayer a public ceremony in which the congregation could and did join. Councils, both national and provincial, insisted on this point, and especially ordained that prime and compline should be regarded as a parochial and almost obligatory form of morning and evening prayer. Yet though it would not have suggested itself to St Dominic to have given up the choral recitation of the Office, it can also be asserted that even if it had he would never have accepted it for his Order, for he was a great lover of liturgical prayer. The biographers of his life tell us repeatedly of his own fashion in devotion. The morning Mass he sang whenever he possibly could, arranging his journeys in such wise that he could be certain of staying at some priory, whether of his own Order or not, in time for the celebration of the sacred mysteries. We read of him genuflecting countless times before the figure of the crucified, repeatedly prostrating himself *in venia* in the presence of the Blessed Sacrament. Bowing, kneeling, standing, every posture of the body, every gesture of it, had, according to his idea, to be welded into the proper method of addressing God. By nature intensely positive, he looked on the worship to be rendered to God as something which claimed the whole of man, which was due from every gift or faculty of soul or body. Hence the idea of serried ranks of men in choir-stalls, chanting the praises of their maker, and elaborating their ceremony by the detailed and punctilious customs of courts, always held his fancy. He is described to us as leaving his stall and passing up and down among the brethren and exhorting them: *Fortiter, fratres*—"More bravely, my brothers"—so he came to look upon Office said publicly as having a formative effect upon the apostle. It was to make him conscious that he was not alone in his huge and adventurous undertaking, that behind him lay a fighting force of prayer. He was trained to look upon his success as achieved not by the mere convincing tones of his eloquence or the elaborate logic of his argument, but by that far more subtle, more intimate, more supernatural weapon, the power of prayer. Out in the plain where the battle raged men cast back their eyes for courage to the hills, and beheld the forms of angel-hosts carrying up before the throne of the Most High the chants of their fellow-friars. Moreover, in a democracy or at least elective form of government there is the danger of a coarsening of the fibres, men who choose their own superiors are likely to lose some of the due reverence for authority, are, indeed, in grave peril of losing their appreciation even of reverence or veneration. Finally, the critical spirit is certain to be enormously strengthened by the mere development of scholastic ideals. The man of culture, especially the clever, brilliant man (the type chiefly prevalent among the earlier friars), the quick preacher, the ready arguer, the swift dialectician, are all liable from their very trade to have scant respect for tradition or for grave dignity or the calm peace of soul. The restless enquiring Aristotle was far more surely to become the patron saint of preachers than the graver and more contemplative Plato.

To avert, therefore, this calamity and to give weight and measure to what else might be simply shallow talk—scientific, perhaps, but not in any sense rich or harmonious—St Dominic was led back to the steadying and deepening practice of the choral Office. It makes, when chanted measuredly, the character unconsciously grave and decorous, gives it opportunity for prolonged contemplation of the mysteries and words of God, and affords it that food for daily sustenance which has nowadays to be provided in the form of set meditation. In those days, to lay and cleric, the Divine Office and the sacred sacrifice completed the fulness of the matter of the spiritual life. Retreats, meditations, private devotions, were not thought much of in comparison with that official salutation of the Creator. Men in those days were led to think of the words of the Scriptures, because they could seldom read them. Now they read the Scriptures so much that they have no time to think about them. But besides the mere recitation of the Divine Office, which was then generally sung in the greater priories but monotoned in the smaller communities (on account of the fewness of the numbers, when so many might be out preaching or on the quest), Dominic added fasts and austerities which were considered even then to place the Friars Preachers among the most severe of the religious Orders of the Church. No doubt the early contact of the saint and his first companions with the dualistic heretics in Mid- and Eastern Europe made them somewhat inclined to go as far as might be possible consistently with the faith in the direction of admitting the doctrine of the evil tendency of material things; and his own deliberate purpose of endeavouring to show that the austerity, upon which the *parfaits* so justly prided themselves, was not entirely unknown in the Catholic body drove St Dominic into making his Order as physically severe as any other. In his determination to grant as much liberty as possible to the will, he was bound to fetter the body; whereas those religious Orders which have surrendered the bondage of physical austerity, have been driven to rivet heavier manacles on the intellect and the will. At any rate, it was the purpose of St Dominic to impress on his Order the characteristic of a hard life. The use of flesh-meat was entirely renounced, linen, still more silk, was strictly forbidden (except for those who might be afflicted by one or other of those numerous skin diseases so frequent in the Middle Ages), the hours of sleep were broken into or rather shortened to what was just necessary for human work. The manner of life itself shall be described in some detail in a subsequent chapter; it is sufficient here to note its character of austerity.

Yet side by side with this fiercer side of St Dominic's ideal, it must be stated also that there ran through the whole a lyric note of gladness. Despite all these regulations to tame the flesh and control the passions by sheer physical privations and penances, or perhaps because of them, we can see, as well from the early texts as from the later development of the Order, that its idea of piety, of holiness, is not in any sense cramped or confined. The Dominican saints have been among the most "natural" of all the models of sanctity whom the Church has raised to the altars. St Dominic himself was instinct with the beauty of holiness. He is found persistently bidding his brethren lay aside all studied and unnatural forms of prayer. His own ardent character with its flaming Spanish idealism wrestled with God in long night-watches and with heavy disciplines to blood, but not only did he not impose these things upon others, he forbade them; for his soul they were as essential as vigorous travelling seems to have been for his physical frame; they were natural to him and therefore made supernatural. But he was content to enrol among his sons men of every type and character so only as they were willing to be fired by his apostolic purpose and to achieve it by the means that he laid down. He insisted upon the choral recitation of the Divine Office, but was no less determined that it should not be so unduly prolonged or chanted so slowly as to shorten the time for study. Everything was to go with a swing, an enthusiasm, yet all the while he was extremely anxious that he should not trespass upon the limits of each man's conscience. When it was reported to him that some of the brethren were becoming scrupulous over the rule and fearful of committing sin by transgressing its least command, he was so moved by this rumour that he declared he would go into every cloister with his knife[1] and destroy every copy of the Constitutions rather than burden men with so galling a yoke. He declared then and afterwards that he did not intend that the rule should bind under sin.

To guard, then, against a too inhuman view of life, Dominic insisted upon the need of prayer to soften and safeguard the intellectual outlook that was a necessary condition of the ideal purpose of himself and his brethren. He drove them to the study of the truths of faith, pushed them on to a study of philosophy and theology, made them instant in exposition and defence, and then to prevent all this from withering the devotional side of their nature by the over-development of the purely abstract interests of the faith, insisted upon a monastic observance of austerity and of the Divine Office. It was no doubt from the experience of his own heart that he found this answer to divine needs. His own boyhood reveals to us rather a solemn little character, detached, austere; his university life forced him still more in upon himself, as he found his books of much more interest than his companions, and disliked their hearty games and frivolous amusements. The only human note that reaches us from that period was his quick sympathy and compassion for the sufferings and sorrows of others; except for this he appears rather a student

than a man of action. The peace and seclusion of Osma succeeded in showing him where his salvation lay—namely, the
chanted Office, the priestly and sacramental life, community
obligations, and interchange of opinion. Naturally generous,
he now became much more human and fuller of sympathy,
more companionable, and discovered that this correction of
his rather abstract tendencies grew out of prayer in its choral
and public expression. Moreover, it is plain, too, that he
found the need of the personal side of faith.

Hence it becomes noticeable how the crucifix came to be
his central means of stirring his devotion and love of God.
The Christian faith comprises a series of statements or truths
revealed by God, and explaining either the inner side of the
divine Being as we note It in the mystery of the Trinity or
the relationship of man to the Creator by the laws of provi-
dence or the destiny and purpose of creation. But these statements were made known to us precisely that by means of
our knowledge of them we might the more closely hold on to
God. The interest of the early Church centred round all sorts
of apparently unnecessary discussions concerning the nature
and being of Christ, and subsequent ages have sometimes
impatiently judged all these to be mere futilities. They are
not futile, for they turn on that very personality through
whom friendship with God himself is to be achieved. Our
Lord was insistent upon the personal character of the appeal
he was making: "Follow me," "Learn of me," "Come unto
me"; and in consequence it is of importance that we should
know him and what he is; nor can any means of acquiring
knowledge of him be safely neglected.

But this knowledge may be said to be acquired primarily
by faith, since it is the revelation of God which must first
unlock to us the inner shrine of himself. Yet this revelation
of himself in definite human terminology and in precise and
careful wording is only the beginning of wisdom. It is not
enough to know all about him; it is further necessary to know
him. Hence as a means of knowledge comes love, for by a
reaction the more we love the more we shall know our friends.
For this reason we find St Dominic deliberately developing
a strong personal devotion to Christ and making his spiritual
life move round that central pivot. There is very little else

apparent in his life of particular fashions of piety, few "devotions," as the expression is. The churches were his shelter, his home, because they housed the Blessed Sacrament. His nights were spent in the presence of his friend, where he remained behind long after the other friars had left the choir for the dormitory. Witness after witness at the Process of Canonisation spoke of these night-watches of his as they had stumbled on him by chance or had overheard his prayers, for, fancying himself to be alone, his positive nature found it easier for him to pray vocally and with gestures, occasionally pausing in silence as though he were listening to another. Prayer for him was an energetic conversation with God, not a monologue. As these friars watched him through the gloom, it seemed to them that opposite to the saint appeared the figure of Christ, the "book of the crucified" in which, according to his own saying, he studied all his sermons. His flaming nature expressed itself in that passionate colloquy between himself and his friend: "At times he smiled and wept"; "He gazed straight in front of him, then lowered his eyes, muttered to himself, and beat his breast"; "He passed from reading to prayer, from the prayer of speech to the prayer of silence"; "Sometimes he would lovingly kiss the book of the Gospels as though grateful to it for some sudden thought of joy, or he would cover his face with his hands, or pull his hood well over it so that he might shut out all distraction and sink more deeply into his thoughts of holiness."

Through these phrases of his fellow-friars we note the same impression made on them, a conversation between the saint and his Master. It was the reality of it which most impressed them, the very obvious way in which he realised the presence of his beloved and made that presence the incentive to his speech. Paul of Venice at the Process noted that St Dominic would sometimes say to his companions as they journeyed preaching: "Go on ahead and let us think of our Saviour"; and Stephen of Lombardy especially remembered his devotion during the canon of the Mass and during the *Paternoster*. It was, above everything else, then, in prayer that he learnt his lesson of untiring energy, and that he tasted the sweetness of friendship with God; and it was precisely in the more personal forms of prayer that he found it most natural to talk. The crucifix, Mass, the Blessed Sacrament, the gospels and epistles, anything that conjured up to him most vividly the personality of our Lord, were to him the easiest means for helping him to pray.[2]

It was for this reason that the devotion of the rosary found in him its keenest apostle. His own way of prayer, consisting, as we have seen, of vocal expressions of love and adoration, was intermingled with silences; it passed from speech to contemplation as it fixed itself on to the character of our Lord. All these elements were united in the rosary.[3] It was contemplative and vocal. It comprised the saying of Our Fathers and Hail Marys which were checked and noted by a string of beads, a contrivance, of course, older even than Christianity, and already widespread over Europe before his time. St Dominic did not invent these things, though it would seem that he popularised them. To him, however, a papal tradition points as the originator of the division into decades or groups of ten, separated by larger beads called *Paternosters*. Under the influence of the Order these chaplets, at this date, spread widely over Christendom, and are to be found carven on tombs, and are from St Dominic's time increasingly alluded to in devotional literature.

But the mere recitation of prayers would be no use unless these could be accompanied by a consciousness of God's presence and of that converse with him that alone gives them a value and makes them efficacious. Hence it was necessary to add the idea of some sort of mystery, some act or scene of our Lord's life, and present it vividly to the imagination so as ultimately to stir the heart to love and worship. The fixing of definite mysteries and of their traditional number was no doubt a long process which it took generations and centuries to evolve and determine, but from the beginning each group of ten was devoted to a particular contemplation. These, therefore, were scenes carefully chosen out of our Lord's life as pictured in the Gospels or as revealed in tradition, and while the lips repeated the most familiar of all prayers, the oldest and simplest of Christian salutations, the mind was supposed thereby to become the better able to hold on to the truth of the scene and gather its full significance. The recitation became almost a mechanical aid to reflection, and the thoughts were thereby freer to concentrate, to abstract themselves, to look before and after. The purpose of the rosary was, therefore, to produce the effect that St Dominic had in view in all his prayers, an intense application of the human soul to the divine personality of Christ.

Finally, it is to be noted that the rosary allows for that pause or silence which Dominic considered essential to prayer. He was the simplest of all the saints in his use of prayer, in no wise hardened by his intellectual activities nor by the fierce work of preaching and its incessant demands upon his vital energy. The action of prayer in his view should never be considered as though it were limited to the human agent, as though man alone was the active partner in it. It must include the silent consciousness of the divine Presence. Indeed, there are many natures, perhaps most, which get their best real comfort out of a strong recognition of God's nearness. For them, for example, the consideration of that sleepless care of his steadily revolved in their minds suffices to bring instant peace. It gives them a due understanding of the ways of God. After all, speech, as such, is wholly inadequate to express our feelings, for the more deeply we feel the less have we to say. Facile and shallow natures bubble over with running comment, have a word here and there to explain all they feel; but deeper natures, when moved and stirred, find that the silence of wonder alone fits their mood. "I were but little happy, If I could say how much" is Shakespeare's way of expressing this generally accepted truth. For this reason, therefore, Dominic added to this simplest of prayers the practice of quiet and silence.

But, it is often asked, why did he insist on an endless repetition of the selfsame words? The explanation is easy enough. In what other way acts love? If it has found its most fitting speech, though it knows even this to be quite inadequate, yet, since it is the best that it can do, should it seek to vary it? So the lover repeats, over and over, his salutation, "I love you." Once, then, we have heard from the lips of our Master the Lord's prayer, and caught from the angel and Elizabeth their welcome to his mother, what better thing can we do than tell these over and over again? "Vain repetitions" is the official judgement of the reform in Elizabethan days; yet what else

was it that in the deepest moment of his agony Christ cried
out to his Father while the sweat broke from him and he fell
beaten to the ground, what else but "the selfsame prayer"?
If such a soul, in its most terrible moment, having found its
best expression sought none other, can less perfect souls be
blamed who follow closely that example? For after all the
very repetition of words, droned heavily out, deadens the
senses to the world about and opens the understanding of
the soul to other and higher planes of thought.

Is there need to add that St Dominic's devotion to the
maiden mother of God was particularly vivid? His friars
were "her friars" (*Vitæ Fratrum*, p. 42) needing and receiving her especial help (pp. 9, 27, 39). Visions were seen, it
was reported, of his sons preaching from books held before
them by our Lady's hands (p. 50); she corrected them, protected them, blessed them sleeping (pp. 52, 53, 60); and
was seen in Cambridge (p. 63) to send fire on them when
they prayed; at death comforted them (p. 280). The spirit
of the saint descended, then, on his children, says Gerard de
Frachet, to sum up all his record of devotion, "so that studying and praying and sleeping they had her before their eyes
and she turned her eyes of mercy ever towards them" (p.
149).

For St Dominic, then, prayer was the simple converse of
the soul with God; and converse is the easier, fuller, when
it is between two friends. The more, then, the mind can
realise the friendship with God, which is the essence of religion, the more facile is the heart's opening of itself, for the
problem of prayer is always how to make God the friend not
only accepted and believed in, but form part of the familiar
circumstance of life. Everything that could help to produce
this truth vividly was made use of: vocal prayer, gestures,
beads; and, since he found that a dialogue of speech and
silence, a chorus of praise, could be more easily secured by a
devotion to the sacramental Presence, it was round the altar
that he grouped his interests. The Mass was the highest expression of it; the crucifix its homeliest representation. The
gospels most wonderfully depict that perfect life and character, and show up against background of hill and lake and field
and village and cobbled streets the moving figure of the true

and loyal friend. Hence the Mass became his most particular devotion; the crucifix his daily companion, his "ever open book"; and the New Testament his favourite study, carried always, learnt by heart, made the textbook of life. "He spoke only of and to God," said a follower of Dominic; and we feel that he did this naturally because God was the central object of his daily work and nightly watching. As Dante observingly notes of him, he was "the athlete" of Christ, "kindly to his friends, fierce to his foes"; he was the "torrential" preacher just because he was "fast-knit to Christ," and he was knit fast to Christ by means of his vivid and intensely personal prayer.

VII

THE ORDER ORGANISED

(1216–1221)

The full value of the statesmanship of St Dominic is nowhere
so apparent as in the organisation and constitution of his
Order. It is necessary to repeat what we have had occasion
already to emphasise several times, that previous to his time
there did not exist a religious Order in the modern sense of
the phrase—*i.e.*, a compact and corporate body with definite
rules running through the whole and organised on lines which
constituted it a perfect unity. Even the canons of St Norbert
and the Cistercians, who came nearest to that as an ideal,
left so much discretion to the individual abbot, that the
union of the monasteries was effected by the meetings merely
of the abbots. The members of each community were normally life-inmates of the local abbey; they even took a vow
of stability, and thus made of a continued residence in one
spot almost a religious ideal; whereas for the Friar Preacher,
it was part of his essential rule that he should go wherever
he was sent, and that the purpose for his frequent changes
need only be the better development of his Order. His no-
tion of life was one crowded with activity, an apostolic journey through the world of his day. To his contemporaries all
this seemed a terrible relaxation of the bonds of discipline.
Matthew Paris, the English chronicler (1200–1259) is full of
complaints that the older monastic theories of religious life

should be thus openly flouted. "They have the world for their cell, and the ocean for their cloister," he wrote bitterly; though, of course, the friars would have been flattered at so true a description of what was their ideal. Again, the satirical writers of that and succeeding ages seized at once on this peculiarity and spoke of the friars as wandering tramps whose notions even of morality had been much blunted by their frequent journeyings. It may well have been that a life free in so many respects led in unworthy souls to much laxity of living; but though it seems more than probable that these writers were describing rather what was likely to take place than what actually occurred, certainly instances are known of evilly-disposed persons concealing, under the habit, hearts which yearned for life on the high-road as an escape from law and order; just as we are assured by mediæval preachers that the same vagrant instinct prompted in some an eagerness for pilgrimages. Yet these known instances are so very few that we cannot reasonably be expected to take them as typical of a common practice. But while Dominic in working out his Order and its organisation created a new type of religious life, he was far from disdaining to walk in the footsteps of those who had preceded him; according to a phrase of Constantine of Orvieto, he proposed to the friars, as the basis of their Order, "what he had seen and known in his youth, and had practised during long years." In his early youth he had been taken often to the great Benedictine monastery of Silos and had seen the full beauty of its life. There was also, close to Gumiel and Calaruega, a flourishing house of the Order of Premontré at our Lady de la Vid, where in 1132 had been established the Norbertine life in its full vigour by a certain Canon Dominic, who died in 1187 when our saint was seventeen and whom, no doubt, he had known. Later, too, when he had left Palencia, he became a member of the Cathedral Chapter of Osma soon after the canons began to embrace regular life, and he had already been with them some years when they obtained official confirmation of their statutes from Innocent III in 1199. From 1200 onwards he is spoken of as "Subprior," and true to his first vocation until the approbation of his new Order in 1216 he always called himself and had himself called "Canon of Osma." He also observed strictly the canonical rule of life, merely adding to it his apostolic work. But this canonical rule was capable of much variety of expression, and St Dominic set to work to think out that form of it best suited to his purpose. On the banks of the Garonne, a few hours' journey from Toulouse, was the ancient Norbertine Abbey of N. Dame de la Capelle, to which he loved to retire from time to time, for the Abbot, John, was his friend. Here in silence he studied the constitutions of Premontré, recalling the life he had seen at our Lady de la Vid in his youth and what he had found also in another Abbey of the same Order at Comblelongue, near St Lizier, where another friend of his, Navarre d'Acqs, had been Abbot before he became Bishop of Conserans. It was, therefore, chiefly from the canonical life of Premontré that he gathered the Constitutions which he proposed to his companions. As the Cistercian life had developed the life of the Benedictines, so the rule of the Premonstratensian canons had perfected that of St Augustine. From them, therefore, he would take all that was most suitable for his object.

We shall examine briefly the primitive statutes of the two Orders—i.e., of Premontré and of Dominic's—to see where the points of likeness and unlikeness lay. We have, on the one hand, the Constitutions of Blessed Jordan as revised at the Chapter of Paris in 1228,[1] only seven years after St Dominic's death, and, on the other, those in use at Premontré in the thirteenth century.

The first paragraph of the prologue is worded identically in both except for the addition by St Dominic of a new principle—that dispensation from the rule, under obedience, was as sacred as the rule itself. These dispensations could be given for three causes—study, preaching, the good of souls: "Because our Order has been specially instituted for preaching and the salvation of our neighbour, our study should tend chiefly, earnestly, and, above everything, to all that can be of use to souls."

This principle, then, shows the idea of St Dominic. All should practise the observances of the canonical life, except where these proved a hindrance to the apostolical life, which was the special work of the Order.

The next paragraph deals with the Divine Office, but instead of the friars at the first signal going to the church for Matins, as did the canons, they were first to say the Office of our Lady in the dormitory, standing immediately on waking.

As regards the chapter of faults, the faults are classified for the friars in the same way as for the canons; similar also are the fast from Holy Cross to Easter, the perpetual abstinence, the quantity and quality of the food, the coarse material for the clothing, the continual silence. So much are these the same in both primitive Constitutions that, with very slight variations, the expressions used are often identical. The same is also true of the chapters of the constitutions dealing with the canonical visitation and the annual general chapters.

A new and essential difference, however, is seen when the day's employment is described, for at Premontré this was to be chiefly prayer and work, and a long chapter is devoted to manual labour; whereas in Dominic's Constitution, this is naturally replaced by paragraphs on study, preaching, lectures in theology, the preachers, the master of the friar students, dispensations for those who study, etc.[2]

Dominic's fervent love of poverty appears next, for while the Norbertine Constitutions say nothing about the character of the buildings of the priory, the friars are ordered to have only poor and humble houses, "their walls not exceeding twelve or twenty feet in height, including the upper storey."

The form of admitting postulants and novices was the same in each case, but the form of profession was again essentially different. "I, Brother ——," said the novice of Premontré, "offer and consecrate myself to the Church of ——. I promise conversion, amendment of manners, and stability to this place. I promise obedience according to the Gospel of Christ, to the rule of St Augustine, and the regular Constitutions of the Order of Premontré, to you Brother —— and to your successors, canonically elected."

But the Friar Preacher, as St Dominic wished it, said, with his hands in those of his Superior after the manner of feudal homage, "I, Brother ——, make my profession, and promise obedience to God, to the blessed Virgin Mary, and to you, Brother ——, Master General of the Order of Preachers" (or "to you, Friar ——, Prior of ——, in the name of the Master General of the Order"), "and to your successors, according to the rule of St Augustine and to the Constitutions of the Friars Preachers, until death."

It was evidently with a marked intention that St Dominic preferred this formula, for to his mind, the Preaching Friar was active and unattached, a knight of Christ and of the Church, always at the disposal of his superiors to wield the sword of the divine Word.

Each, therefore, made profession to our Lady and promised her a special obedience, which Humbert de Romans said was not done in any other Order.

The ending of the Constitutions was originally the same in both: "To secure peace and unity throughout the whole Order we have written this book, which we call the book of our Institutions."

Dominic, then, intended the Order of Preaching Friars to be a mobile body, and, in consequence, a democratic one. It seems to be a law of history that the more stationary life is, the more autocratic will be its theories of government. The "unchanging East" is the home for despotism, whether beneficent or otherwise, whereas the movement of trade, the turmoil of the cities, the noise of traffic, the frequency of change, lead to the rise of democracy, and as these progress in volume and importance, to the extremes of radicalism. Once the means of transit become increased and quickened, a people grows correspondingly interested and alive to its own government, and thus induced to take even a larger share in it. The "free cities" of mediæval history are types of what was commonly noticeable among the more active religious Orders. The more they make their home in the towns, the more democratic grows their rule; the further and further they retire into the country, the more completely do they put themselves into the hands of a single life-superior. At least, this was the natural development of religious life in the mediæval times. Moreover, in this direction, St Dominic had as well the influence of Spain to guide him, where first in Europe the towns were drawn into the national assemblies or parliaments; even his own equable temperament that loved his fellows with a love of comradeship made him opposed to any perpetual superiority either in his own hands or in those of others. One abbot he instituted; but never another; and after that single experiment he became consciously wedded to a system of representation and election. Driven by the purpose of his work, by his own national custom, and by his personal character, he elaborated his theory of government on a basis of popular rule.

Following the custom of Premontré and of the Knights Hospitallers, he broke up the Order into provinces or nations which were themselves composed of groups of houses. Each house was to contain at least twelve religious, and to be governed by a prior; each gathering of priories (not less than three) within the limits of a nation or kingdom was ruled by a prior provincial; and the whole Order of linked provinces was administered by the Master General. The very name "master" shows how impregnated this branch of the friars was with study as its first principle. The office of the Master General was at first for life, and so remained till the nineteenth century, when it was cut down to six years and finally raised to twelve. As at present constituted the prior provincial holds his position for four years and the prior conventual for three. All these positions are elective. For the election of the prior, the qualifications of the voters have varied slightly in history, but the present law is practically only a modification of the method in use in the time of St Dominic. Each cleric who has passed through his normal course of studies and who has been for nine years a professed member of the Order (profession following after exactly twelve months noviciate) has the right to take part in the election of his prior. The qualifications which the prior himself must possess are that he must have been professed for twelve years, and, to be prior in a cathedral city, must further have obtained a degree in theology. In the election he has to secure a simple majority; but if he is also one of the electors, a member of the community which is electing its own superior, he must further have in his favour a majority of one over two-thirds of the whole number voting. The object of this last provision was to prevent any election being carried through by an elector voting for himself. Further, the name of the elected has to be forwarded to the prior provincial for confirmation.

The prior provincial himself is chosen by the votes of his subject priors and by one member of each community, who is selected for this purpose. At the provincial chapter, which will shortly be described, the priors, then, are gathered, and with them each a socius, or companion (whom each priory has of its own free will, without suggestion or interference by its superior, sent to represent it). On the same principle as in the case of the priors, these elect a provincial, whose confirmation must also be sought at the hands of the Master General. Finally, the Master General himself is elected by the votes of the prior provincials and of officials (called diffinitors) provided for this special purpose by each several province. Thus it will be seen that the hierarchy of the government of the Order is based on the general principle of election, and side by side with this it includes the system of representation. It may indeed be stated that Dominican government in legislative and in executive rests on these two ideas; first, that all holding office of superiority should hold it by the free votes of those whom they are to govern; and secondly, that in the selection of rulers (other than the merely local superior of a local house) election shall itself be carried through by means of representation. Further, this also must be recognised, that, in the Order of St Dominic, the superiors are only an executive. They have no power of themselves to make laws, but are empowered only to administer the laws of the Order or province, and to see to it that these are carried out by their subjects.

For along with the election of individual superiors must be recognised the system of legislation by chapters. These alone have the right to make and to unmake the laws of the Order. At the beginning of the Order, both in the provincial and general chapters—that is to say, in the parliaments of the province and of the whole Order—certain regulations, originally made as to the number present and as to the place where these were to be held, have been subsequently changed. But the practice of to-day has the venerable antiquity of nearly seven hundred years, for it dates from the years which saw also the definite shaping of the English Parliament. How far it is possible to maintain that Simon de Montfort and afterwards Edward I were influenced by the Dominican model and in what measure consequently the English representative system is due to the fertile genius of St Dominic may be studied in detail in the *Dominican Order and Convocation* by Ernest Barker.[3] It is sufficient to note here that they are both symptomatic of thirteenth-century feeling and show the large spirit of freedom which in Church and State was at the moment influencing public life.

At the provincial chapter, held at first every year (subsequently every four years), there came together the priors from each house. These were, as has been seen, elected by the communities chiefly for their powers of administration. If to these alone had been committed the law-making power, it was feared they might favour authority at the expense of freedom. Hence with them came also a socius selected by the community, not for any governing capacity, but simply to represent in the assembly the voice of the governed. He was of importance only during the few days which the chapter lasted, and as soon as his labours were completed he sank back to his ordinary position of subordination. In this way a man of ideas who had not sufficient evenness of character to be able to govern with success might yet very aptly represent a community and suggest new laws on behalf of the ruled, or modifications of old ones. These two elected representatives come from each priory within the borders of the province. Their work is to elect among their number or among the whole province four diffinitors and the prior provincial, and to these five were left the work of legislation. Immediately after electing these five delegates the rest return home; and the chosen representatives devise the legislation required, either new regulations or amendments to actual rules. The *Acta* or decrees published by these are then forwarded to the Master General, who confirms them or not, according as in his judgement they agree or conflict with the existing laws of the Order or are for the good of the province or its harm.

Besides these two members from each house, places in the provincial chapter were also given to masters in sacred theology and preachers general (both titles assigned for work done, the first being obtained by examination and fourteen years of teaching, the second by strenuous labours in the fields of the apostolate, and both granted by the Master General or the Chapter General only at the request of the province).

The Chapter General was constituted on the same principle, for it was attended by provincials and by a representative of each province elected precisely for the immediate purpose of the chapter. Yet there was this difference in their arrangements. The first chapter of the new Master General is necessarily elective, and to it come both provincials and diffinitors (the official name borne by the representatives of the province) in order to elect and also to make or amend laws. At the second, it is the diffinitors alone; at the third, the provincials alone; at the fourth again diffinitors with provincials, since according to present law this will be an elective chapter, as it terminates the twelfth year of the Master General's office. It will be seen, therefore, that now authority is equally divided between the provincials and the representatives of the province, but in the times immediately succeeding the death of St Dominic, when the Master Generalship was a life-appointment, every third chapter was of provincials alone, and the other successive two were of diffinitors alone. An elective chapter from the beginning combined both elements, but it was only held on the Master's death or resignation or translation to some higher office in the Church. Also, at the same period, instead of the provinces sending one representative to the general chapter, and the priories sending one representative to the provincial chapter, in both cases two were sent. It was only after 1360 that the present custom became law.

Finally, two other curious practices must be recorded; one, that whenever provincial or prior or diffinitor attended such a chapter, he was accompanied by a socius whose business it was to take his place, should he through sickness or death be unable to perform his duties. The socii were understudies to the principal players. The other, that each law had to be passed by three successive chapters before it became part of the Constitution, nor could a statute be removed from the Constitutions unless its removal were sanctioned also by three successive chapters. Thus, in every case there could be no undue nor hasty legislation forced through in a spirit of panic, nor could there be a law brought in simply in favour of, or at the expense of, authority, for a subsequent chapter composed either solely of provincials or solely of diffinitors would always be able to block it by refusing confirmation. The first reading was called an *Inchoatio*, the second a *Confirmatio*, the third a *Constitutio*.

Above the general chapter stood the *Capitulum Generalissimum*, which has met, however, only twice in the history of the Order, in 1228 and 1236. It stood as equivalent to three Chapters General, for it comprised the provincials and two diffinitors. Its decrees, therefore, at once had the power and binding force of a Constitution.

This in brief, without mention of unnecessary details, sums up the organisation of the Order. It will be noticed at once how broad was its spirit of freedom and how deep its trust in the principles of democratic rule. It is clear, too, that it was precisely this love of liberty which St Dominic himself bequeathed to his Order; nor is this wonderful when the search for truth is realised to be the purpose of his foundation. For truth itself, complete, intact, can never here be achieved. Age by age, generation by generation, men approximate to it, but always it is just beyond them, a pillar of cloud and of fire, out of their reach, an ideal accomplished only in Heaven. Yet those who so vainly search and follow it have this measure of success, that though they miss perfect truth they achieve perfect freedom. For to cling to truth, to serve its interests alone without thought or fear of consequences, to follow blindly its steady gleam, in no way influenced by personal advantage or professions of friendship or loyalty even to a failing cause, to attack falsehood even when it is an inaccurate statement by one's own side, ends surely, by the very essence of the courage which it requires, in true freedom of the soul.

Yet it must not be imagined that this democratic or elective and representative system is without dangers or even faults. It is always liable to become utterly inefficient. By its very nature it is capable of a great loss of strength and vigour. The simple fact that a superior is subject to election may bring with it the tendency for him to suit himself to his electors and to be, in the phrase of Lafayette, "a leader just so long as he is content to follow his men." Moreover, not seldom disunion, or perhaps more accurately distraction of forces, is a mark of democratic rule. Nor have these defects been wanting in the history of the Order. It is evident that at periods

in their story the Friar Preachers have suffered from their
own form of government. Had they been more straitly organised in the hands of a single ruler, whose power was autocratic and who was not responsible to the whole community,
had the Master General been able to appoint his subject
provincials, and had the provincials themselves had the power
to nominate the priors of the houses within the limits of
their jurisdiction, it cannot be doubted that sometimes a
very serious decline in zeal or learning or observance might,
not improbably, have been stayed, for freedom, like friendship and the sacraments and all things noble, can become a
danger through its abuse, a danger the more perilous and
degrading because of the sacredness of that which is abused.
Yet to those that live under its shadow, liberty in electing
government is too blessed a thing to be put aside even at the
risk of inefficiency. With all its inherent weakness, for them
it mates better than any autocracy, however beneficent, with
the independence of human reason and the strengthening of
human will. Under the driving force of autocratic government
a man may indeed work harder and with greater success, but it
is doubtful whether he is himself any the better for it. He
may even, if he be a Christian apostle, bring in more souls to
Christ, yet he may not have added thereby one cubit to his
spiritual stature. After all, it is not what a man does, but what
he is, that is of supreme importance in the sight of God. For
just as the faith would ever insist upon the huge power of
prayer and trace back more of the Church's triumphs to her
contemplatives (cloistered or in the worldly places) than to
her active missionaries and leaders, so it may well be, indeed
certainly is, a better thing to arrive at the footstool of God's
throne alone yet a masterpiece, than, surrounded with other
rescued souls, to come oneself less loving and more ill-made.
True self-culture is the purpose of faith and hope and love.
Hence Dominic would himself, no doubt, willingly have admitted that a democratic system of organisation might in
certain cases prove terribly inefficient, and that it brought
with it, despite certain excellencies, certain great defects.
Still in his eyes those excellencies would appear to outshine
their shadows, for the defects are defects in external work, but

the excellencies lie in the soul. Democracy may mar results, but it makes men.

Searching, then, after truth, the Order of St Dominic, in its sympathy with each generation's attempt at formulating principles, with its steady devotion to discover the eternal verities even in systems of error, heresy, and revolt, has never quite caught up to the object of its quest. It has sought for truth, but it has found freedom.

During the discussion of the orthodoxy of the writings of Savonarola, Fra Pietro Paolo d'Arezzo, O.P., Master of the Sacred Palace, rose to defend them. In full congregation, he was attacked by Cardinal Gaddi: "Father, your office as Master of the Sacred Palace is to defend the Apostolic See, and not assail it." "My Lord Cardinal," replied d'Arezzo, "my office is to defend truth, and I should hold myself dishonoured were there to go forth from this Palace anything contrary to truth."

That is the bequest of St Dominic to his children, to search for truth and to become free.

VIII

HIS COMPANIONS

The character of St Dominic naturally drew friends to him, and especially the young. His whole outlook on life, perhaps, appealed to them, his austere demand for generous devotion, his even-temperedness, his joyousness, his ready gift of companionship, his spirit of democratic government by which youth could and did climb instantly to places of importance, his genial breadth of view that tolerantly made a place for everyone in the Order. His "boys," indeed, were almost a standing jest of the period, and many were the gibes levelled at them by their fellows and the reasonable criticism of their elders. Old dames, we read, trembled for their moral dangers, and even at times accosted Dominic to point out the impropriety of sending them to preach in twos and threes without an elder friar in charge "young and handsome and in so comely a habit";[1] but the saint only laughed at their objections, and prophesied great things for their work. Could his "boys," then, fail him when he had so openly defended them? He had believed in them, and he taught them in consequence by God's grace and our Lady's help to believe in themselves.

Of that little band with whom he began his missionary enterprise we have really hardly any record: Stephen of Metz, one of the earliest names that appears, a devoted follower chosen by St Dominic as his socius in the journey to Rome after the dispersal of the brethren on August 15, 1216; another was William Claret, the skilled businessman to whom Bishop Diego left the temporal cares of the preaching group after his departure into Spain, the hard-working and laborious prior of Prouille, to whom the quiet convent life meant more than the apostolic vocation, and who ended his days as a Cistercian monk. Then there were the two Toulousois, Peter Seila and Thomas, of whom the first became later prior of Limoges and eventually was appointed inquisitor and died in 1257. Earlier possibly were John of Navarre and Dominic the Little, both Spaniards, probably members of Diego's little embassy or later recruits to the mission after the Bishop's return, and dispatched to the aid of the saint. Of these two, John was in many ways the particular favourite, the spoilt son, and his witness at the Process is the most touching of all. Dominic the Little was sent to Spain in 1217 with Michael Uzero, but neither of these could brook the opposition they met with, and both returned discomfited to St Dominic in Rome. The saint, however, himself was not to be intimidated by disaster. He took his namesake back with him to Spain at the end of 1218 and left him at Segovia, only, noticing his timidity, he replaced the little man by Friar Corbolan as superior of the priory that dates from February of the next year. Round Laurence of England legend has grown; but our real knowledge of him is confined to very little indeed. Of Mannes, we have fuller information. After the dispersal he began his career by a stay in Paris, probably in 1218 returned with his brother to Spain, passed through Segovia and Gumiel d'Izan and Osma, and then settled at Madrid as confessor to the nuns. He continued quietly in this office till his death, and though he did not, like William Claret, join them in life, lies buried among the Cistercians. The Paris expedition had been headed by Matthew of France, evidently a man of some consequence. He was a friend of Earl Simon de Montfort, and, being a native of the Ile-de-France, was looked upon as likely to secure for the friars a creditable place in society. He was not put in charge of the studies of the house, for his gifts were the practical gifts of the organiser. Indeed, he leaves on us an impression of pompous solemnity, for his temporary position as head of the Order was not relished by his brethren, who had been spoilt by the perfect genius of command shown by Dominic himself. Further, we read of Suarez Gomez and Peter of Madrid, both very successful in Portugal. Gomez founded his first priory under the munificence of the Infanta Sancha, whom he had known at the court of her brother, King Sancho, and he devoted much of his energy to this noviciate house of Santarem. Altogether he combined great facility in preaching with high talents of administration and an inspiring influence on others. Raymund of Penafort dedicated a volume to him as "Prior in Spain of the Order of Preaching Friars," for Dominic appointed him provincial of Spain at the chapter of 1221. The Kings of Castile and Portugal both turned to him in disputes that had troubled them, so that we gather an impression of him, as of a vigorous and kindly character, the inspirer of others (for St Raymund is not the only writer in Spain who dedicated his works to him), gentle, decisive, an organiser, the founder of many priories, precise and detailed in his observance of the rule and Constitutions. All these must, indeed, have been older than mere "boys" when they began their preaching career.

William of Montferrat, who had known St Dominic in Rome in 1217, went after to Paris, where he was received to the habit by the saint in the June of 1219. He accompanied the master to Rome that same year in July, and in consequence at the Process had plenty to say on the life of his "blessed father." The Provençal Bertrand of Garrigua[2] was again another to whom St Dominic seems to have spoken very openly of himself, or at least as openly as he ever did, for he was not one who unburdened himself to his companions with much ease.

Of Hyacinth and Ceslaus we have already had occasion to speak, their eager, impetuous hope that sprang so easily in that age and that made them offer themselves to convert the whole of northern and eastern Europe. The traces of this gigantic campaign long survived, but the swaying fortunes of the Near East, where Christian and pagan fought each an endless crusade, soon made ruin of the priories built and established in the lifetime of these two apostles. From Greenland on the American continent to Kieff the white habit was spread, while on the Russian borders, and through Poland to the effete and menaced kingdoms of the South, both Greek and Latin, convent after convent rose, centres of propaganda and ultimately of martyrdom, for the Golden Horde, which eventually blocked the trade route of the north-east, and reduced the busy market of Nijni Novgorod to years of silence, began their huge incursion by wholesale massacre. Hyacinth was the more adventurous of the two and made good his ambition of becoming a famous missioner; he lived to extreme old age and, despite many perils, died in peace. Ceslaus, on the other hand, was not so hardy a character; after some years of co-operation with Hyacinth, he, along with Henry of Moravia, moved over to Bohemia and began a very large priory at Prague, intended by its founder to be the centre of missions still further afield. Within Ceslaus' lifetime martyrs had gone from it to Bosnia, Prussia, and Pomerania. A convent of the second Order of Nuns in Prague also claimed him as its founder, and hither came Margaret of Austria, the repudiated Queen of Bohemia, to find a place of rest at the ending of her life. Ceslaus himself laboured in the countries about Bohemia and Moravia, visiting Prussia, Saxony, Pomerania, and Silesia. The number of his converts, given in figures perhaps too high for accuracy, is evidence at least of a fruitful apostolate, due in great measure to his attractive character. Amazing innocence of life is repeatedly mentioned in the early accounts of him as his most endearing characteristic, and he is described as attracting to him the friendship of many young men. No doubt in those wild countries where paganism still flourished more brutally than elsewhere in Europe, such a Christian attribute as purity must well have proved a magnet to the young. The simplicity of his teaching added to this, for he particularly devoted himself to explaining the fundamental truths of faith, the mystery of the Blessed Trinity and the divine maiden motherhood of our Lady being the chief burden of his preaching. A lovable old man, he seems to have been gentle, devout, yet vigorous, in his dying speech confiding all his religious "to the merits of Jesus Christ," without which "the exercises of the cloister were wholly vain." Hyacinth died on the Feast of the Assumption, and Ceslaus on that of our Lady of Mount Carmel in 1242.

But the friend who most influenced St Dominic in his latter days[3] was undoubtedly Reginald of Orleans, as his name is now usually given. A brilliant lecturer on Canon Law in Paris in 1206, he secured the benefice of the deanery of St Aignan in Orleans in 1212, and came in 1218 to Rome to search for some means of living a life "of preaching and poverty." A Cardinal who was devoted to him referred him to the new Order and particularly to "the master who preaches God's Word at this very moment in the city," to whom, therefore, Reginald hurried off. The presence of the saint in the pulpit stirred him, "his beauty and his eloquence," and as soon as the sermon was done the impressionable young professor spoke to Dominic and revealed, under the moving influence of the impassioned speech, the inner secrets of his heart. Dominic in turn was carried away by the charm and fervour of the Frenchman; they seemed meant for each other. Yet for the moment Reginald hung back. His impetuosity was restrained, for as soon as he had left the saint's presence the magic of its personal element failed him. All his old uncertainties about his vocation returned and so plagued him that he got driven into a real fever. To his bedside Dominic came daily, and discussed the problem of his calling, planning, indeed, with Reginald even the future of the Order. The scene as described in the primitive life irresistibly recalls the figure of Hurrell Froude, the same flaming temperament, the inspiring genius, the brilliance, the wasting strength; Reginald was driving Dominic more and more away from the respectability of the canonical life, and urging a more poverty-stricken following of Christ. A vision of our Lady followed, in which the Mother of God appeared to him and anointed him after the fashion of the extreme unction of the priest. One of the hospitallers, who was nursing him, witnessed the same vision. She promised to return the third day to repeat the miracle. Reginald was now at peace, for she had bade him join the friars, and had shown him the white scapular which these were now to wear. This was her answer to their discussions, and Dominic was to be informed of her wish. As she proceeded to the ceremony of anointing, she recited, as it seemed to him, these words:

May your loins be straitened by the girdle of chastity,
May your feet be shod in preparation for the Gospel of peace.

On the third day Dominic was present, and himself saw
the vision and heard the words and the command. He was
convinced and obeyed; and Reginald rose up immediately
"cured alike of his fever and of concupiscence."[4] This last
had haunted and tortured his memory, and made him fear
the impossibility for him of such a vocation as Dominic had
proposed. Reginald at once "made profession," but had to sail
immediately after to the Holy Land with his Bishop. On his
return Dominic dispatched him to Bologna (the world-centre
of Canon Law) to build up the newly founded priory. He
reached that city on December 21, 1218, and began his mission at once. "Bologna is in flames"[5] was the epigram in
which Jordan of Saxony summed up the success of the new
preaching. Like Dominic, and indeed like Jordan later, the
appeal of Reginald was entirely to men. We read of none else
than men present to hear him, but of men in crowds. Particularly he urged on them the religious life,[6] and that with
such power that often professors and students stayed away,
terrified of what he might make them do under the spell of
his eloquence. Moneta, for example, a converted Paterine,
later one of the famous scholastics of his day, and already a
man of some eminence, a professor of the arts, steadily refused to go to hear him for fear of what should happen to
him, and was only at last dragged off to the priory by the en-
thusiastic boys to whom he lectured. Even then Moneta
insisted on their going to Mass first at St Proclus' Church,
and stayed on for two more Masses in the hopes of putting
them off their project, though ostensibly agreeing to accompany them; but as soon as he whispered, "Now we can go,"
they marched him off at once to the Dominicans. The densely
packed little church of the Mascarella allowed them just to
squeeze inside the doorway, but after such emotional misgiv-
ings, Moneta was already in the most receptive frame of mind.
At the first phrase he was a captive; and like Reginald himself
hardly much more than a year before, when the sermon was
done, he moved up through the crowd to see the preacher,
opened his whole conscience to him, and at once made pro-

fession: "As his numerous duties as professor could not be immediately resigned, he continued to wear his ordinary gown for a year, though he spared no effort to secure fresh recruits and to induce them to attend the sermons. Sometimes it would be one person, sometimes another, and whenever he managed to get a novice to join, it seemed to him each time as though he was himself taking the habit."[7] Roland of Cremona, even more famous than Moneta in that age wherein thought, purely abstract thought, was considered as great a thing as action, was another of those whom Reginald drew to the Preaching Friars: "He was a well-known professor of the University, an eminent philosopher, and the first of the Order who taught theology publicly in Paris," says Gerard de Frachet,[8] whom also we have quoted in describing the calling of Moneta. Roland's story must be added just because it shows the curious state of men's minds under the influence of these first friars: "Driven by the Holy Spirit, he had come alone and of his own initiative to the door of the priory. He was brought into the chapter house and there, as though drunk with the Holy Ghost, he without further preamble begged to be received to the habit. Formerly on feast days, clad in rich scarlet, he had made merry with his friends in feasting, games, and all kinds of pleasures. When at night he came to himself, he would under the prick of grace ask, 'Where is now that jolly banquet? What has become of all that mad gaiety?' At last, under pressure of the thoughts of the fleeting character of pleasure and its swift turning to sorrow, he entered the Order, where he served the Lord for many years in wisdom and holiness."

In the spring Reginald moved the priory to St Nicholas of the Vineyard, receiving to the Order its rector Ralph,[9] who gave witness later to the life of St Dominic at the Process of Canonisation. At the end of 1219 Reginald was sent to Paris; but he does not seem to have been so successful there as he had been at Bologna. He died almost immediately after his arrival, broken with his incessant work of preaching and his fierce austerities.[10]

Now, the story of Reginald's life had been told in Paris to the friars by Dominic himself in one of his conferences while Reginald was still in Bologna, and one of the young men

present (for the university public were admitted) was a young
Saxon, Jordan by name, the most affectionate and generous-
minded of undergraduates. He secretly was fascinated by the
saint, but shyly held aloof, daring only to creep into these
meetings unobserved and listen on the edge of the motley
crowd of hearers, though on occasions he ventured to confess
to Dominic and to ask his advice on his future calling, for already he was a subdeacon. But he was tortured, as Reginald
had been, by doubts against his vocation to the Preaching
Friars, for he too had fallen a victim to incessant thoughts
of evil, such as we know, from other sources, plagued so
many of the Paris theological students. In those tempestuous
days the university found the holiness of Christian life very
difficult indeed where a crowd of young men were gathered
together, away from home and the peaceful influence of home
affection. To Jordan, then, Reginald's story and cure appealed, and on Reginald's arrival in Paris Jordan felt em-
boldened to ask for an interview.[11] His favourite study was
the mathematical sciences on which he has left some treatises,
but he realised his own wonderful power of sympathising
with and attracting all kinds of people. The question, therefore, he had to answer was whether as a cleric he should continue his scientific studies and become a professor, or whether
he ought to make use of his gifts of attractiveness by becoming a priest and by throwing himself into the apostolic life
for which the friars stood. Dominic had already urged him to
become a deacon, but he still hung back, chiefly through his
friendship with a fellow-student, Henry of Cologne,[12] "whom
I love in Christ, with an affection that I have never felt towards anybody else, a real type of perfect and honourable
manhood, the most graceful and charming soul in all the
world." Henry refused to be moved by this friar-enthusiasm,
and though reluctantly, indeed, under Jordan's persuasion,
he went to confession to Reginald, he was no more convinced
than before. On his return from confession, the two thought
to solve their difficulties by taking the Bible and opening it
at random, an ordeal by lot, *sortes biblicæ*, as it was called.
The passage they lighted on was the verse of Isaias: "The
Lord made me to hear his voice and I did not resist him, I
went not back." This finally convinced Henry. Both were re-

ceived into the Order together on the same day, and continued their friendship till the end. Jordan was soon appointed to lecture on Scripture at Paris in place of Roland of Cremona, which he did "with great charm and distinction." He subsequently became provincial of Lombardy in 1221, and succeeded Dominic himself as master of the Order the same year. The instant acceptance of him by the Order as its general is an extraordinary tribute, not only to the character of the young German, but above all to the strength and power of Dominic's influence, for there were many others in the Order who might have been thought to have claims to succeed the saint. We have noted how both through Dominic's own influence and through the persuasive eloquence of students like Reginald men had flocked to the young Order from the most famous universities of Europe, had left the chairs of professorships that it was the ambition of all learning to fill, men old in the labour of teaching, preachers of note in the cosmopolitan world of Christendom in the thirteenth century. These still remained when Dominic came to die. Moreover, at his death there survived almost all those who had lived under the saint's obedience from the beginning, who were early companions of his missionary days, who had shared with him the counsels of Bishop Diego, who had borne uncomplainingly the heats and turmoil of the long years from 1206 to 1221. Some, indeed, were to survive to the Process of Canonisation in 1233, and these must have been in full vigour when the succession had to be settled. Matthew of France had already borne rule and might seem to have claims to the mastership; John of Navarre was Dominic's best-loved son; Bertrand was the constant companion in his last days; Ventura had anointed him and watched him die. Mannes survived in Spain. Hyacinth held the North under the spell of his eloquence. Even in Rome itself there were friars of importance; while, above all, in remote Prouille lingered William Claret, the co-partner with Dominic in the work of the foundation, who had shared with him the responsibility of the preaching band when Diego left them for Spain, who knew better than any the inner history of the Preaching Order, and who had followed step by step the gradual development of its ideal. Yet none of these was chosen to fill the saint's place, but Jordan only, the youngest of those in office, hardly more than two years a friar, only recently a German student in Paris, who had been made provincial in Lombardy.

What made the friars turn to him, and wherein lay even in his shy yet eager youth the promise that the future did indeed display? It is very difficult to understand the motives of the choice, for no hint is given that Dominic had singled him out by name.

Yet among all that band of followers whose characters in any fleeting way are shown us, Jordan most nearly resembles Dominic particularly in those gifts by which as a master he would have to hold the Order together. He had the same superb physical constitution, the same endurance of endless travel; he had the same vitality, energising power that moved those under him to put forward their very finest efforts; he was touched with something of Dominic's austerity and tempered with even more of Dominic's own joyousness, a man of personal charm and tact, to whom, as to his master, friendship was the real support of life; a ready and flaming preacher whose particular fortune it was to gather to him the younger members of whatever congregation he addressed. Oxford, Paris, Bologna crowded the churches where he preached and followed by hundreds (when his Lenten course was done) into the Order he so incessantly described as "Heaven's Gate." But more than all, the general acceptance of Jordan witnesses to the successful organising work of Dominic, who transplanted from Spain a democratic method of government and set it up, greatly daring and more greatly trusting, among the most cosmopolitan assembly then in Europe.

The Spaniard was followed by a German, who reached the succession by the votes of French, Spanish, Roman, English, Provençal, and German friars, gathered in Bologna under his leadership.

God's greatest gift to man in the order of nature, and almost the greatest even in the supernatural plane, is the gift of making and securing friends; and judged by this, Dominic was indeed blessed by God. The loneliness of boyhood ripened in community life into that mixture of charm and reserve which attracts and holds men's hearts; the radiance that the first biographer noted in the Osma days shone steadily to the last. Weakened by his travels and the fierceness of his fever, hollow-eyed and restless, he still from his bed of death charmed the people about him; even when death had hushed in silence the perfect voice and stilled the beautiful hands and stiffened the slim figure and dulled the fine and shining eyes, his haunting presence held the group together and made them, without question, accept the way of life he had ordained.

IX

HIS PORTRAIT

It always makes him more vividly real to us and even leads us the better to a complete understanding of his character, to find a true portrait of a saint or indeed of any man in whom we are interested. In some indefinable way the inward grace of the soul shines through the outward show of human appearance; not that moral evil and bodily beauty are incompatible, but that goodness of life will deepen beauty and remove from ugliness something of its repulsiveness. The difficulty in many cases is to be sure that the portrait left us is a real likeness and not merely imaginative or ideal. Yet by some trick of luck we do happen to have some true portraits of the long-since-dead. Through sculpture, for example, we know most of the great men of antiquity "in their habits as they lived"; on the other hand, of the very earliest Christian period we are chiefly at a loss, except for unsure frescoes or later mosaics; of the subsequent and especially of mediæval periods we have often most excellent records, showing without shadow of doubt the forms and features of those whose characters we know.

In St Dominic we are singularly blest. There are several representations of him that rightly claim antiquity, three, indeed, at Bologna and one at Gaeta; but the picture that is the best authenticated is that which is preserved in the Church of San Domenico Maggiore in Naples. It is painted on wood, over a surface of jesso. The figure is grave and austere, the attitude natural, the folds of the drapery are severe and noble, the whole atmosphere of the picture full of simplicity and strength. From it we recognise at once the "strong athlete" whom his contemporaries have described for us, that vigorous nature of his, not destroyed by grace, but rather deepened and strengthened by it, wholly different from those pale and bloodless "saints" presented to us by religious art that seems leagued with the enemies of Christianity to show the faith of Christ as a weakening and enfeebling influence, producing types of humanity physically and morally unfit.

No other picture of St Dominic can produce more proofs nor more decisive proofs of antiquity. There is a tradition, which there is no reason to doubt, and which can be continuously traced, that this painting was brought to Naples in 1233 by Thomas Agni da Lantino, who founded the Dominican Priory of San Domenico Maggiore in 1231, and as prior gave the habit of the Preaching Friars to Brother Thomas of Aquino, and died Patriarch of Jerusalem in 1277. This tradition of the picture is supported by direct evidence and particularly harmonises with the date of 1233 claimed for it, for since it was precisely in that year that the Process of Canonisation took place and the translation of the relics occurred under Jordan of Saxony in the presence of the general chapter of all the friars, it is likely that portraits would have been painted for devotional purposes in the Order. Further, the severe and simple style, the dignified attitude, the flat colouring in perfect accord with the artistic methods in use in Southern Italy at that period, the entire absence of symbolism, all combine to bear out the traditional history and date of the picture. The face is rather Spanish in appearance, wears the short beard which we are told he allowed to grow so as to be able to journey to the Tartars, and shows that complete tonsure of which other records assure us.

It resembles very closely the description dictated in old age to Sister Angelica by Sister Cecilia,[1] one of the nuns whom St Dominic had transferred from the Trastevere Convent to St Sisto. "He was of middle height, his countenance beautiful with little colouring, his hair and beard very fair, and his eyes strikingly fine. A certain radiance shone from his forehead and from under his eyelashes attracting love and respect. His hands were long and beautiful, and his voice strong, noble and sonorous. He never became bald, and always retained his perfect tonsure, though the white hairs of age had begun to appear."[2] Theodoric of Apoldia, writing in 1288, carries on the same tradition. He also refers to Dominic as of middle stature, slim and beautiful, of slight colouring, with his hair and beard fair and rather tending to red; and notes equally that "radiance" from the saint's forehead to which the nun has referred, adding the same phrases about his "joyous and happy expression," his "slender and beautiful hands," his "voice sonorous as a bell," his "perfect tonsure," and its "few white hairs." Certainly as we watch carefully that pictured face we have no difficulty in recognising the austere character which even in boyhood seemed so solemnly set. Gregory IX, who as Cardinal Vgolino had known him intimately, describes him in his Bull of Canonisation in 1234, "while still young in years, he already bore in his boyish heart the studied gravity of old age," and Amizo of Milan,[3] prior of Padua, in his deposition on oath at the Process, uses a significant word when he says that Dominic "in all his acts and speech was very mature." The note of austerity was, as we have already had occasion to remark, partly natural and partly deliberately assumed. "His frugality was so austere that, except on rare occasions and out of consideration for the brethren and others who might be at table with him, he ate nothing but bread and soup," says the Abbot of St Paul of Narbonne, who had preached with him in Languedoc. "I have never seen a man so humble or one who despised the glory of the world and all that belongs to it. He despised himself greatly, and reckoned himself as nought. He passed whole nights without sleep, sighing and weeping for the sins of others. I have never heard or known of his having any other bed than the church, if a church was within reach; but if there was no church near he lay on a bench or on the ground or the planks of the bed which had been prepared for him, after carefully removing first all the bedding." A witness recorded that the saint while preaching the Lent in the Cathedral of Carcassonne in 1213 was "living upon bread and water alone, and never making use of a bed." John of Spain (or of Navarre) also speaks of his terrible austerities: "Master Dominic had the discipline administered to him and scourged himself besides with an iron chain." Ventura who had assisted him in his last agony reported that "on his arrival at a priory, he, unlike most men, did not retire to rest, but always, calling together the community, spoke to them of God and sought to increase their fervour of divine love." Even when Master General he would retire to his cell to receive the discipline and "had it administered with a triple iron chain." The judges of the Process asked Ventura how he knew this; he answered: "I know this from a religious from whom he asked this service." "Never did the blessed man (he adds), even on his journeys, eat meat or any dish cooked with meat, and he made his friars do the same. The only exception he made was in favour of the sick and old, who were allowed to eat meat in the infirmary and were not obliged to the rule of rigorous fast." "Outside the towns," says Theodoric, "it was his custom to walk barefoot, sometimes among stones and sharp pebbles, often through thorns and briars, so that with feet all sore and bleeding, he would exclaim in holy joy, 'This is part of our penance!'" Neither hardness of the road nor widespread floods ever prevented him from any journey, and when on the road he never let anyone else carry his cloak or his books. If he could find a religious house in which to shelter, he turned into it for his rest, following the rule which he found there; if no priory or monastery was near, he went to a hostelry or lay out quietly under the open sky. "He rejoiced in tribulations," says one witness. "He begged alms from house to house," said another, "and when in one place he was given a loaf he received it on his knees." It was a sacrament of love, and he knelt to receive it with "Domine non sum dignus" on his lips. "None was more instant than he in watching," says the primitive life. "Seldom in his cell, keeping vigil in the church, and when too tired any longer to keep awake, then stretching himself along the altar step . . . very truthful and hard living, avoiding delicacies, living on a soup diet, having his body under control." Silence, too, was a law of his life, as Prior Ventura of Bologna bore witness, keeping the monastic solemn silence after compline "even on the road." He slept clothed and shod, even as he walked during the day, removing only his hose. He observed the fasts rigorously when travelling and cared little what he ate, taking absently whatever was given him except meat, and often so tired that he slept sitting at his meals.

Yet this austerity was well-tempered with a joyousness that increased steadily as life went on; yearly he grew more boyish, more light of heart, more gay, as the roadway of age slipped by him, and as he found that others depended so much on him for their courage. "He fasted every day, yet was careful that his friars should eat well because of the fatigues of travel," said Paul of Venice at the Process. "He shared the common life and rigorously practised fasting and the other observances. If he perceived any infraction of the rule, he punished the delinquent gently; and even when the penance imposed was severe, it was inflicted with such eager kindliness that no one was ever indignant or sulky. . . . To others he very gladly gave dispensations, to himself never," were the comments of another witness. Says Jordan of Saxony: "None was ever more joyous than he, and none a better companion"; he adds, "Nothing disturbed the even temper of his soul, except his sensitiveness to pity and compassion." "He was always radiant and joyous, except when moved to compassion by some misfortune of his neighbours," almost verbally repeats Sister Cecilia, looking back across sixty years at the hero of her girlhood. "He accepted insults, curses, and abuse with patience and even joy," says the Abbot of St Paul of Narbonne. "With tender kindness he comforted those good fathers who were sick, wonderfully patient with their infirmities. Generous and hospitable, he gladly bestowed upon the poor all that he possessed. He loved the faith and he loved peace, and as much as in him lay, he loyally furthered both." "Sixteen years ago," deposed William of Montferrat in 1233, "the present Pontiff, then Bishop of Ostia, offered me his hospitality, and in his house I frequently met Brother Dominic, who was at the time attached to the Papal Court [no doubt during Dominic's long sojourn in 1217 to secure the due authorisation and development of his Order]. This gave me the chance of getting to know him, and (adds William, always a little pompous in his careful diction) his society gave me much pleasure and I began to love him"; and Gregory, himself the Pontiff, in the Bull of Canonisation, spoke of Dominic as "bound to us by ties of close friendship when we were in a humble state." This kindness and joyousness were noticeable in him equally with austerity. Along the road as he travelled he had a word to say to everyone, hardly able to pass a group of pilgrims without going over and greeting them, helping to land some poor English wayfarers who had tumbled into a stream, making himself understood by a band of Germans who could not speak a common tongue with him: "He tried to talk of God to almost everyone he met on the highways." When in his Spanish travel his disciples lost courage and left him, he is noted in the primitive life to have been not "indignant" but "compassionate."[4] He prayed for them, and most of them returned to him. Indeed, the author himself later declares that it was quite natural for Dominic to be full of sympathy, and he makes use of a choice expression, saying of the saint that "he took all into the arms of his wide love and was loved himself in turn by all." Prior Ventura, who gives us a very austere picture of the saint, also witnesses that Dominic was "never uncharitable, always affectionate, and quickly made you feel at home," was "always good to talk to when you were in trouble"; everyone who went to him "always came away consoled." He was strict, of course, and punished, but so sweetly that no one could ever be other than content. Prior Amizo agreed heartily with this: "A kindly consoler of everybody, and especially of his own brethren." John of Spain spoke of him as "pleasant to rich and poor, to Gentiles and Jews, of whom there were very many in Spain. Everyone loved him except the heretics," and he gives instances of this. The first band of preachers "had money and horses and great warm coats," and it was only gradually that Dominic got them to give these up; "They were given to the Cistercian nuns of France." The saint, he says, "had no proper sleeping place, and yet was always joyous"; and Ralph, who was rector of St Nicholas in the Vineyard when it was handed over to the friars, was sure "he often slept sitting down." He too it is who assures us that at the first general chapter of 1220 Dominic resigned his mastership as unworthy of the office, and only consented to take up again the burden when diffinitors were appointed to help in the

legislative work of the Order, and so relieve him of something
of his toil.

Kind indeed he was, full of happy memories for others,
such as when he carried back from Spain to Rome in 1219
across half Europe for each of his dear nuns of St Sisto a little
spoon of cypress wood.[5] Austere and kindly, flaming with
enthusiasm yet even-tempered, confident and decisive, yet
willing to accept the plan of the majority, he seems to stand
easily above his brethren, the leader whose wise foresight
made possible the philosophic generalship of Aquinas, the
missionary zeal of Hyacinth Odrowantz, the eloquence of
Vincent Ferrer, of Savonarola, of Las Casas, of Lacordaire.
The secret of all this is not far to seek; his greatness in planning his Order came because he sought always for freedom of
soul, to control the flaming Spanish temperament, to hold its
fervour carefully in subjection, to be unhampered and un-
afraid. He had early refused the bishoprics of Beziers, of
Comminges, and of Conserans, declaring "he would sooner
take flight under cover of darkness with no belongings save a
staff than accept the episcopate"; nor was this because of
false humility, but, as his friend the Abbot of Boulbonne
bore witness at the Process, because Dominic wished "to be
free to concern himself only with the Friar Preachers and the
nuns of Prouille. This was his work and his mission and he
would take no other." At the first general chapter and at all
the meetings he was never self-assertive, though always sure
of his own policy and opinion; "confident of his own appoint-
ments," says the primitive life, "though others wondered and
were in doubt"; dispersing the brethren at 1216 against the
advice of Earl Simon and the Archbishop of Narbonne and
the Bishop of Toulouse, saying to them (as John of Navarre
remembered), "Don't contradict me, I know what I am doing." He held steadily by his own judgement when he had to
decide, but in other matters allowed his brethren as much
say in the affair as himself: "As long as the meeting lasted, he
was merely one of the friars. If he took the first place it was
only in abstinence, vigils, fasting, mortification, setting himself above none save unconsciously in holiness." To secure
the same spirit of freedom as we have already recorded it,
"he declared in the chapter house at Bologna for the comfort

of the weaker brethren that even the rule does not always bind under sin, and that if others were likely to think otherwise he would go into every cloister and cut them to pieces with his knife," and, adds Humbert, "the friar who heard this from the saint's own lips repeated it to me."

It was in freedom's name that he recalled to their observance the early friars who had rejected the scapular and retaken the canon's surplice, misliking this talk of visions on the part of feverish subjects like Master Reginald, and keeping their moneys and travelling on horseback.[6] The chapter of Bologna was held to settle the matter, and it was Dominic's personal character that carried the day against these friars of Toulouse. He surrendered office and made himself one among his brethren; but he first sequestered all the moneys of these southern friars and sold their horses in auction in the public square of Bologna to pay for the upkeep of the chapter.[7]

By sheer personal character he secured a law forbidding the possession by the Order of landed estates; "Lest the office of preaching should be impeded by the care of earthly goods they were in future to have only gifts of ready money." They could retain their churches and priories, but nothing else; and when Oderic Gallitiani handed over to the prior of Bologna an estate, Dominic saw that the property was restored and the deed of gift torn up in the sight of the whole chapter.[8] "Except for the sacred vessels no gold or silver would be allowed," nor silk permitted even on the altar. Mosaics were forbidden, even marble tombs and indeed tombs at all prohibited in the friars' churches. Humbly mendicant, they were to subsist on alms even for their daily bread. John of Spain,[9] witnessing in 1233 at the Process ("come the Feast of Augustine next, would be eighteen years from my clothing in the habit as near as I could tell"), still remembers this intense spirit of poverty and the sense of freedom which its observance brought, though he has not forgotten his escapade before going to Paris that very same year, to which we have already alluded.

His work, then, of preaching was from the very first Dominic's determined vocation. "He was so fervent a preacher that day and night in churches, in houses, in the fields, on the roads, he never ceased to proclaim the Word of God, enjoining on his brethren to do the same and to let their conversation be of God alone" is the witness of one of the Cistercians in Languedoc, and tradition, already old in 1240, tells of the high commission granted him for this in 1217. "One night, when the blessed Dominic was praying in the presence of the blessed Sacrament in St Peter's in Rome for the preservation and extension of his Order, the Most High deigned to show his approval thereof. A vision suddenly showed him the two glorious princes of the Apostles, Peter and Paul, coming towards him. Peter solemnly gave him a staff and Paul a book, while together they commanded him: 'Go and preach, for unto this has God chosen thee,' and they showed him his children scattered two and two the wide world over evangelising it."[10] Certainly he realised the double commission. On his journeys, always afoot, he carried simply his staff, his cloak, and some books: "He never entered any house where hospitality was given him without first saying a prayer in the church, if there was one in the place. When the meal was ended he retired to a corner under the window, where he read the Gospel of St Matthew or the Epistles of St Paul, which he always carried about with him. He would sit down, open his book, cross himself, and then begin to read attentively." His influence is marked in the early legislation of the Order wherein it was laid down that "the hours of the Divine Office are to be recited briskly and with precision, so that the brethren may have longer time for study. . . . Those who are successful at preaching shall be employed in no other office. They are to devote themselves to reading and study rather than to the chanting of responses and anthems."[11] Ralph, the last secular rector of the vineyard church in Bologna, expressly declared at the Process that "no one who was suited to the office of preaching was ever given any other official work to do by Dominic." He had certain very clear notions as to what preaching entailed, saw to their being carried out, and would never consider any Friar Preacher justified in his life who was not incessantly devoted to study. No opportunity was missed by him for insisting to his young followers on the need of the study of the arts and sciences, and especially of theology and the Bible: "I can affirm it, for I myself have heard him say so very often," and it is recorded that he lectured in Rome on the Epistles of St Paul and in Bologna on the psalms and canonical epistles. It would seem, perhaps, to us as though he had hardly time for study in a life so eagerly lived, so crowded with untiring labours, but even when he was ill he read and was read to, and thus managed to secure food for his day-long meditations.

He made no secret of his desire to attract particularly the brilliant university folk to his Order, precisely because he knew that in that age of wild speculation and eager discussion this was the type of worker that could best secure his object, that from their ranks could alone be successfully gathered the preachers most fitted to move and convince that generation of hardy thinkers, inflamed by the passion of logic and captive to nothing else than the free expression of the truth. He himself had followed with his six companions the lectures of Toulouse, had dispatched the first band of his sons to Paris, the second to Bologna, and went deliberately in 1220 to Padua "because of the university that was there."[12]

He was, however, careful not to neglect the devout side of religious life, never so hard a student as not to have time for long and absorbing prayer. "I have never seen a man to whom prayer was more habitual," was the witness of the Abbot of St Paul. His presence in the choir has already been commented on; his resolution to allow neither the tiredness of travel nor the incessant demands that his organisation of the Order made on him ever to relax his punctual attendance at the choral recitation of the divine Office. He was indeed anxious to form a body of preachers, tireless and learned; yet no less did he desire that their type of sermon should be founded upon an austerity of temper, a solid grounding in the Scriptures, a monastic strength of purpose, a character tranquillised and stilled by the chanting of psalms and antiphons. The Friars Preachers were always to remember their canonical—that is, clerical—status.

Further, "as soon as they awake and rise, the friars shall together in the dormitory recite the matins of our Lady according to the season of the year and then proceed to the choir." Then at the watch of midnight (between twelve and three) matins were to follow, and the round of prime and the other hours duly recited according to the various times that the liturgical year arranged. A community Mass when the earliest office was done was to be followed by all, priests, students, lay brethren; but not till a little later was the idea of meditation as a formal and common obligation introduced. It was taken for granted that both in the church or the cell the friars would be found in contemplation of the deeper truths of faith. An age that had few books and few opportunities, as we would judge, even for private writing, was necessarily an age that was perfectly able to spend the greater part of the day in sheer thought and contemplation. The temperament then to be found everywhere would have wondered at our powers of continuous reading and would have been astonished to discover how little time or opportunity the individual now has for personal thought. Hence to them the great works of the day were thought and prayer. The library and the church are expressly stated to have been the places in which the friars were first looked for. It was only when these were searched in vain that the brother was guessed to be in his cell. Eager-minded though people then were, they had far more than we of the patient and still contemplative spirit of the East; they thought more than we, pondered more, and were more active in their mental concepts and in consequence more violent in their practical conclusions. Once printing had been introduced and reading became more common, religious Orders found themselves forced by a sheer love of sanity to protect the individual against himself by insisting upon a certain definite amount of time being daily devoted to deliberate meditation.

Each friar was permitted to have in his cell a crucifix and a statue of our Lady, "so that at prayer, at study, or at rest, he might contemplate them and remember himself to be in turn contemplated by Sovereign Mercy: for the image of the crucified is the book of life spread open, to which our eyes are to be raised and whence cometh our help."[18] Herein Dominic strove to soften and make pliable the nature that under the impulse of study might stiffen and grow hard. Emotional himself, stirred quickly to compassion, "weeping easily and making others to weep," he knew that the real convincing preacher must not disdain to train his whole being for the work. There can be no thorough science of the art of preaching except the man prepare thoroughly for the task. It was just here that Dominic was essentially the creator of the school of the apostleship of the Word.

By temperament, as we have tried to show, he was pre-eminently fitted for the task. His solemn childhood had made him perhaps rather reserved and a lover of quiet and retirement. His mother's care, his family life in "happy Calaroga," the seven years of home training, the influence of his brothers, older than he and filling his early childhood with the talk of the priesthood, accustomed him thoroughly to the studious side of life. His brother Mannes, of whom alone we have any details, was of a very quiet disposition; his last years in Spain were spent, as far as can be told, wholly at the disposition of the nuns at Madrid; the elder brother remains little more than a mere name; the sister has slipped out of all record. We find the boy, therefore, living at home in a quiet household of good family until he reached the age of seven. Then the next seven years under his uncle's tutelage would hardly have done much to show him any more lively vision than the peaceful round of study and prayer. He had the level of the bleak Spanish plain to hold his eyes with scanty traces of the civilisation which after the peace of the Dark Ages then had begun elsewhere to emerge to its blossoming period. The boy was still shut in by life's hazard, dreaming the hot days through, wandering up the edges of the hills in the early spring, a thoughtful watcher of still life.

The *studium* of Palencia to which he then was sent was becoming famous at this very period, and nearly ready to receive official commendation and final approval; but its growing crowd of students failed to jostle out of his personal love of silence and quiet the solemn boy of fourteen whose whole character and temperament made him hold closer to his books. Already the clerical estate had called him, and the services of the Church were becoming of personal interest. He watched them so as to be able in his own time to take due part in them. Meanwhile the canons of his own Diocese of Osma were being re-organised, receiving new regulations; his Bishop offered the boy a canonry to support him through the period of his studies; he accepted the dignity and was bound now to the service of the Church. When the studies were over the young graduate, opening out now into a very sympathetic but peace-loving recluse, passed into the cathedral cloister. The company of the canons, many of them young like himself, called out all that was best in him. He overcame amid congenial surroundings the shy hesitation of his boyhood and became changed into a radiant centre of community life. Perhaps for the first time he lived close up against people of his own age; before he had been the youngest at home, then in the arch-priest's household a mere boy, later the silent student shrinking from his fellows at Palencia; now he found himself actively engaged in prayer and converse with friends and equals. His real joyousness showed itself, in Jordan's phrase, now expanded to the sunshine, of this new and gay-hearted life.

The embassy broke the evenness of his canonical round of simple duty. The Bishop, like all the world, having found him a most delightful companion, took him with him on his journey. The shy boy now grown man was driven to convert the world, and discovered this at Toulouse at his first opportunity. The scene of this showed him the opening of a new career: the dimly-lit hall, the other guests asleep, the Bishop amusedly listening to the eager arguments of the subprior who knew so little of life, the innkeeper who thought he knew all types of human nature fascinated by the freshness of this cloistered soul. It was Dominic rather than his arguments that led the man home to the faith.

His first success and the kindly interest of the Bishop both combined to push him on to the career of preaching from which he was never to look back; Dominic was not only admirably suited to the work, but never ceased to train himself for it. He had had the finest education for this very work; trained by the exact sciences to marshal proof and to collect converging arguments, he had the facility of scholastic memory, the readiness of speech, the rapier stroke of argument, which all found their growing perfection in his disputations with the heretics. His presence was attractive, his voice beautiful, his slender hands instinct with graceful gestures, his slim figure retaining its youthful litheness under the physical efforts of his continuous travel. Further, he had immense strength of bodily endurance, the flaming heart of Spanish enthusiasm, the radiance of character which alone could make tolerable those long days of endless walking. Joyousness sprang out of the physical energy, the sleepiness that found no bed too hard, neither the bare ground, nor the altar steps, nor the carved stalls. He loved the company of others, particularly of the young. His radiant purity drew to him the generous hearts of all youth and made his very hands cool of their passions some tempted undergraduates.

Austere and hardy, able easily to bear fatigue, affectionate, touched quickly to tears and laughter, devoted to others, full of a lively gaiety of heart, he had the very foundation of the preacher's gifts. Well educated, happy in his memory, trained to argument, he never neglected any means of keeping himself perfect for the work. He was abstemious in his food, singing loudly with his clear voice across the hills, gesticulating even in his prayers with indefatigable energy; he swayed and carried audiences of every kind.

With all an artist's temperament and emotion he had the gifts of organisation and command; decisive, humble, lovable, his only weakness was too zealous an eagerness at first in publishing (of course, with the best of all motives) his austerities and even pretending a holy hypocrisy.

But that passed, and out of the strenuous pressure of life he awoke to sincerity and strength. The dreamer of Fanjeaux saw before him the level plains of his whole career when he planned his friars and Prouille. His portrait shows us that dreamer whose dreams came true, and reveals line by line the hidden power that faced them in marshalled pageantry "through the gates of horn."

HIS DEATH

(1221)

From December, 1220, to May, 1221, St Dominic spent in
Rome, making use of his nearness to the Papal Court to obtain the various privileges which he found from experience
his friars and the Sisters needed.[1] Already forces were being
engineered against his project by local authorities, who ob-
jected to this energy of preaching, and who considered its display a tacit criticism of their own lack of apostolic spirit.
The primitive life tells of a priest much disturbed over these
new religious, wondering whether or no he should give them
welcome, and opening the New Testament at random, and
being reassured by happening on that passage in the Acts of
the Apostles that recounts the coming of the Holy Spirit on
the family of Cornelius in the house of Simon the Tanner,
"for they heard them speaking with tongues and magnifying
God" (Acts x. 46); and again we read of Conrad, Bishop of
Porto, when he was apostolic legate in Bologna,[2] troubled as
to whether the preachers were really to be encouraged or not,
and asking for a book to be brought him that he might try
by lot to discover their purpose. Presumably the book brought
was the Missal, the handiest of all in that place, for the line
that his finger touched occurs in the Mass Preface for feasts of
our Lady: *Laudare, benedicere, prædicare*. It was wonderfully appropriate—"*to praise, to bless, to preach*"—so that the

Bishop could no longer hesitate in the presence of the friars. The phrase has since been accepted as its motto by the Order.

But these stories, though they end so happily, show the rising of the attack that was to be launched against his sons after St Dominic had gone; Jordan of Saxony met it by prayer; Raymond of Pennafort, who succeeded him, was broken by it and resigned; John the Teutonic and Humbert de Romans organised against it the brains of the Order, joined forces with the Franciscans, who were also threatened by it, and deliberately steered straight at it till it failed in courage and went under. But already St Dominic had experienced its beginnings and referred to it as he died. During this last winter in Rome he met again Foulques of Toulouse, with whom he had faced his earliest days of trouble, and settled with him the affair of the tithes of the diocese; these he renounced, for his brethren were no longer diocesan missionaries merely, but had made the whole world their home.

In May Dominic set out for Bologna, and on the 30th held the second general chapter of the Order.[3] It was the final organisation of the Preaching Friars that was now definitely settled; Dominic had realised, and so had all, that something must be done to hold together these scattered priories and link them into an organisation; and it was here that the system of visitations, largely in use among the Norbertines, was finally taken over. Moreover, the erection of various provinces was determined on and the provincials themselves chosen; six of these provinces already existed, and for these it was merely a matter of settling their boundaries and announcing to each priory within each radius its immediate superior; but the last two provinces were only as yet planned:

SPAIN	*Suero Gomez.*
PROVENCE	*Bertrand of Garrigua.*
FRANCE	*Matthew of France.*
LOMBARDY	*Jordan of Saxony.*
ROME	*John of Piacenza.*
GERMANY	*Conrad the Teutonic.*
HUNGARY	*Paul of Hungary.*
ENGLAND	*Gilbert of Fraxineto.*[4]

Paul was a student in Bologna at the very time, a man of some brilliance in the university, and after the fashion then prevalent he offered himself to the saint for the work in his native country, and was received to the habit and immediately dispatched home. Success by way of preaching and eventually of martyrdom followed the establishment of his priories, and his great foundation of Alba Royal long remained a missionary centre for all the south-east of Europe, carrying the faith to Transylvania, Serbia, Wallachia, and the Tartars of the Dnieper whom St Dominic had so earnestly hoped himself to convert.

Gilbert, as we have already shown, was a student in Bologna, and had no doubt offered himself for the English foundations; and as Paul's recommendation for Hungary was that he was himself a Hungarian, it does not seem improbable (as a later tradition asserted) that Gilbert also was a native of the island to which he was sent. Perhaps, then, we may call him Gilbert Ash. His success was, of course, speedier and more lasting than Paul's. He landed in England with the Bishop of Winchester, was introduced by that prelate, Peter des Roches, the leader at the English court of the foreign baronage, to the Primate, Stephen, Cardinal Langton, who was the leader of the English baronage. The Cardinal invited Gilbert to preach in his place that very day, and he so well acquitted himself that the Cardinal promised the little band of thirteen friars his high patronage. The first priory was pitched at Oxford on August 15, 1221, where schools were immediately opened on the site of the present Town Hall; within a century over fifty priories were dotted over these islands. Moreover, as confirming the statement of the primitive[5] life wherein it is said that St Dominic's decision on the fitness of men for various offices never required to be changed, when in 1230 the English province, fully established, had its first elective provincial chapter, Gilbert was chosen as provincial prior, although nine years had elapsed since he first came as superior and since the saint's own death.

In June, Dominic, though feeling ill, went off to Venice to confer with Cardinal Ugolino on the fortunes of the Order,[6] and returned in July to Bologna, feeling weary and yet, says the primitive life, "of indefatigable spirit." The very night of

his arrival home in the heats of mid-July he was busy discuss-
ing the affairs of the convent with Ventura, who had recently
become prior, and with Rudolfo, the procurator, of the little
house. He had already fever on him, and both these, who
were tired after their long discussions far into the night, tried
to persuade the saint not to go down to the midnight matins,
but to take what sleep he could. Thinking they had succeeded
in inducing him to retire, Ventura and Rudolfo themselves
went to sleep and woke next day to learn that Dominic, on
leaving them, had gone down to the church to prayer and
had been at matins. But in the morning the fever returned
with increased violence, and after Mass the saint threw himself on a sack of wool to try to get some rest and sleep. The
heats of that summer were intense and added to the discom-
forts of the fever; so that after some hours the brethren carried him out to a little country place on the high ground
above the city, near the Church of St Mary of the Hills.
Here he lingered for some days, "joyously and sweetly" in-
structing the novices and consulting with the older fathers on
the future of the Order. Lying high up amid the great ter-
races of vines, he spoke of his early life and the whole story of
its peaceful beginnings; to those who watched by him, he re-
counted stage by stage the establishment of the Order, the
days of Toulouse, the founding of Prouille, the opposition of
Pope Innocent, the choice of the rule, the kindly welcome of
Pope Honorius, and the final establishment of that Order to
which his whole life from the beginning had unconsciously
turned. He could see the design of his wandering life now,
working back in spirit from Bologna to Rome, and to Provence, Osma, Palencia, Calaruega. During the sleepless nights
he mused over his past and made his public confession to
Ventura and the elders. Among all his many graces, it was his
guarded chastity that at that last moment he seemed most
grateful for: "God has in his mercy kept me till this day in
pure and unstained virginity. If you desire this blessed gift
of God, hold yourselves apart from everything that can con-
jure up evil, for it is by watchful care in this that a man is
loved by God and revered by man. Be eager in your service of
God; strengthen and widen this new-born Order; increase
your love of God and your keen observance of the rule; grow

in holiness." But even as he spoke, he remembered how purity was a virtue that needed silence in its defence, and how, perhaps, it seemed like his old habit of boasting to be speaking of it at this last hour, and so he forced himself also to say: "Though God's grace has preserved me from all stain till this moment, I must admit that I have taken much more pleasure in conversation with young women than I have with old." Then still afraid, his voice sunk to a whisper: "Brother," he said to Ventura, "I think I have done wrong in speaking of my virginity aloud. It would have been wiser to have been silent." The troubled, anxious soul, how shall it ever learn when it should speak to help and when it should hide the secrets of the King? At the last going of a great leader, should his followers be told of the inner struggles that none has ever guessed? Would it comfort them to know how human really he has been? Or in that last moment, should they think of him still as someone unalterably above them? Yet as Dominic whispered of his virginity and of his pleasure in the fresh beauty of eager youth and made the faltering confession of a long enduring war, we cannot believe that the radiance of that joyous countenance was less bright.

Then he made even more gravely his last bequest. "These are, beloved ones, the inheritances that I leave you as my sons, have charity among you; hold to humility; possess voluntary poverty." It was of poverty that he then went on to speak, as he had already spoken of chastity, and he solemnly laid his curse on such as should in any way interfere either by gift or acceptance with the poverty he desired to be continued among the brethren; from the hill he could see the unfinished walls of the new priory which he had forbidden them to build, a suitable text for that last sermon that he preached. He was told that the Monk-Rector of St Mary of the Hills was eager to give him burial in the church, for no one feared to talk of death to him as he lay "facing the lonely way." His answer was the request at once to be taken back into Bologna to die. A lover of the brotherhood in life, in death he equally desired to be among them; "Under the feet of my brethren" were the only directions he ever gave for the placing of his tomb. Back he was carried to the city, borne slowly, for every now and then it seemed he might die on the journey, so frail had he become, that the least jolting of the stretcher made his heart fail him; but "the indefatigable spirit" even then carried him over that tiresome journey.

The lasting of his life was now only a question of hours. Rudolfo never left him, wiping from the still joyous face the sweat of death. As he began to enter into his agony, Dominic could not but notice the tearful eyes of those who stood about him; and the old courage and laughter prompted an answer that still consoles his sons: "Do not weep, beloved ones; do not sorrow that this frail body goes. I am going where I can serve you better."

A foolish questioner still thought of the body and its future and asked where he wished to be buried. "Under the feet of my brethren" was again his answer. Why would they trouble him thus at the last with the disposal of the frail body? It remained, of course, but he would be gone. Why waste his last precious moments with idle questioning?

Rudolfo noticed the approaching end, and Dominic, equally conscious of it, sent for Ventura and the others. "Father," said the prior to him, "you know how desolate and lonely we shall be. Remember us in prayer before the Lord." But already Dominic had begun his remembrance of them. "Holy Father, I have accomplished thy work with joy. Those whom thou gavest me, have I kept. To thee now that my care of them is failing I give them back again. Behold, I am coming to thee, Father in heaven." Then he turned to Ventura to get ready for the prayers for the dying. They were just about to begin, when he bade them wait a little, perfectly conscious, dictating every movement, indomitable to the last. "I am going where I can serve you better," he repeated; service had been his life on earth, it would be his life in heaven. When he had said this he made a sign, and said quite audibly, "Begin"; and at his word, they began the prayers of recommendation for a departing soul. Ventura was nearest to the saint and thought afterwards that Dominic was saying the prayers with them; his lips were moving certainly, though he could not catch the words. At the *Subvenite*, "Come to his help, ye holy ones of God; come out to meet him, ye angels of God, taking his soul, and offering it in the sight of the Most High," Dominic repeated the sonorous phrases of that tremendous command over death, and lifting his feeble hands as though to join in that last appeal, opened his eyes, sighed slightly, and was dead. It was six o'clock in the evening of Friday, August 6, 1221. The saint had hardly completed his fifty-first year.

"He died in Brother Moneta's bed because he had none of his own; he died in Brother Moneta's tunic, because he had not another with which to replace the one he had long been wearing,"[7] is the comment of one of his earliest biographers. It sums up the detachment and poverty of his life. It pictures graphically the wandering mission of the greatest of Friar Preachers.

After death Rudolfo proceeded to dress the body and get it ready for burial, and the brethren watched the dear remains, chanting the psalter by the bier. But somehow no one now felt any of the heaviness that they had supposed would follow upon his death; radiance shone through the whole of life, and joy was in their hearts.

At the funeral Cardinal Ugolino presided, hurrying from Venice for the purpose, and with him were the Patriarch of Aquileia and several bishops and abbots. Miracles even already began, and people spoke of a fine tomb and offered silk adornments for the body; but the friars would have none of those things. They did not want a crowd of people always about the place, nor did they want anyone to accuse them of making money out of their saint, so a wooden coffin was got ready and the body placed in it. It was sealed by the Cardinal and then buried in the Church of St Nicholas of the Vineyard, "under the feet of the brethren."

Miracles, of course, followed, and these the friars could not prevent. For example, we have sworn testimony to the case of an English undergraduate, Nicholas Wood of Worcester Diocese,[8] ill from that Michaelmas of 1221 till Pentecost following, so that he could not walk without a stick, and eventually compelled to keep to his bed as his leg had withered, who turned in his despair to the intercession of the saint. After a fortnight of the pain, he ordered a candle to be made of the length and thickness of his body and promised

to devote himself "to God and the blessed Dominic." While
he was being measured for the candle, from the head to the
loins, and the man was holding the tape to pass down from
the thigh to the feet, Nicholas suddenly jumped up crying
out he was cured, and ran to the church which was "an arrow-
shot away." By 1233 these miracles were so common and the
popular devotion was so intense that the church was found
too small, and it was considered necessary to rebuild it; consequently the body had to be disinterred. While the new
church was being built, however, the tomb of the saint was
not in any way protected; but it was determined to erect over
it a new tomb which should be better worthy of the remains.
Jordan of Saxony presided at the translation on May 24, 1233,
in the presence of very many friars who had come to Bologna
for the general chapter, and of the bishop of the city, the
Archbishop of Ravenna, and others. The aged Pope, who had
reached his hundred years of life, and who was none other
than Cardinal Ugolino, now Gregory IX, had dispatched the
Archbishop and several bishops to witness for him the opening of the relics.

Jordan himself describes graphically the ceremony. He tells
of the friars "in an agony of doubt, praying, trembling, ex-
cited." They wondered whether "so long exposed to the rain
and to the heat, in a common grave, would not the body of
the blessed Dominic be found in the natural state of corrup-
tion and of decay?" Anxiously the friars pressed forward to
have their doubts settled; but when the stone that overlaid
the grave was raised, there was no need for pressing near to
see in what state the body was, for a "sweet and delicious
fragrance spread from it, such as suggested rather the spiced
perfume of the East than odours of the grave. The archbishops and bishops and all those present, filled with joyous
wonder, fell on their knees, praising God who had thus strikingly glorified his chosen one." Jordan goes on to tell how he
removed the bones and placed them in a pine-wood reliquary,
which in turn was laid within the fine new marble tomb. But
the civil magistrates of Bologna insisted a few days after upon
the tomb being again open for veneration, and as the chapter
still sat the whole body of 300 friars, led by the Master General, passed by, one by one, "placing a last kiss on the withered

brow of their father." For long afterwards the church was
filled with fragrance and the hands that touched the poor
dried bones carried for days the perfume of that presence. But
the tomb which Jordan had so choicely erected was soon considered itself too mean for the "gentle perfect knight" whose
remains it covered. In 1267 was completed a new sarcophagus
resting upon a row of pillars, the work of Niccolò Pisano and
a Dominican of Pisa, Fra Guglielmo. This still remains the
great ark which holds the relics. Along each side are two bas-
reliefs divided by statues, on the front, of our Lord, and on
the back, of our Lady; at either end are other bas-reliefs.
These six reliefs represent the principal scenes from the
saint's life, and are made up of sculptured figures, of which
each has been carved with delicate grace and care. Just two
hundred years later, in 1469, the tomb was further added to
by the addition of an upper portion, covering the lid of the
sarcophagus with exquisite worksmanship, by Niccolò di Bari,
known in consequence of this masterpiece as Niccolò dell'
Arca. This part of the tomb is crowned with a majestic figure
of the eternal Father and surrounded by St Dominic and
various other saints, an angel in prayer, and the descent from
the cross. The work was, however, still unfinished when Michael Angelo (whose own brother was a Dominican and who
had followed the fortunes of Savonarola) took it in hand and
completed the upper part by carving two figures of saints and
a superb kneeling angel. Fifty years later again, in 1532,
Alphonso Lombardi carved the base of the tomb with reliefs
depicting the birth of St Dominic, the Adoration of the
Magi, and the triumph of St Dominic.[9]

But the translation under Jordan of Saxony in 1233 and
the flood of miracles that followed stimulated Pope Gregory
IX to hold a commission of enquiry into the life of Dominic
and to begin at once the Process of Canonisation. This was
opened by a papal decree of July 11, 1233, under the presi-
dency of the Archdeacon of Bologna, the Prior of St Maria del
Reno, and a canon of the Trinity. It sat in Bologna from
August 6 to 31, and took the depositions on oath from those
witnesses who had best known him, a touching and human
record to which we have already many times over referred
and from which we have quoted many passages. Further, at

Toulouse a second commission collected evidence from many who had an even longer knowledge, remembering Dominic in his days of early missionary labour, some of those "younger women," no doubt, whose conversation had pleased the weary and travel-stained preacher, and who were still devoted to him and his memory. Garrulous old women their depositions seem to make them, but their hearts were hearts of gold. They told of his austerity, of his incessant journeys, of the hardiness of his life, and, womenlike, they protested their efforts to care for him, noticing the two points that all women would at once have been unhappy about, his scanty food and his threadbare clothing. Both he thought little of, and over both they were concerned. They had mothered him and tried to get him comforts, had persuaded him to eat with them, had made and mended his clothes, had covered him with extra blankets as he slept. Naturally he was a saint in their eyes. The record is touchingly human, for we see through it the personal affection he inspired, yet also something of that reserve that formed part of his nature. They comment on his joyousness, his playfulness, his naturalness of temper, but you feel all the time as you read their sincere declarations that they knew him as someone apart from them all. He was a friend to them all, but you feel as you read that *his* friend was God.

By a Bull issued at Spoleto a year later, July 13, 1234, the Pope declared as a result of the enquiry that the sanctity of Dominic was proved, and what had been merely the devotion of friends could now be allowed to the whole Church.

The feast day was fixed for August 5. It could not be celebrated on August 6, the anniversary of his death (the usual day chosen for a newly canonised saint), for that was already occupied by the Feast of the Transfiguration; later on, the Festival of our Lady of the Snows (the dedication day of St Mary Major in Rome) was transferred to August 5; so that now St Dominic's day is August 4, a day memorable indeed to our generation as the anniversary of war.

The Pope thus witnesses to the life of Dominic: "Whilst he was still young in years, he bore in his boyish breast the heart of a mature man; choosing a life of continual mortification he sought the Creator of all life; dedicated to God and

vowed a Nazarene under the rule of St Augustine, rivalling
the zeal of Samuel for holy things, he recalled the holiness of
Daniel by the zeal with which he chastened his desires. Strong
as an athlete in the way of right and justice and the path of
the saints, never departing from the teachings and the service
of the Church militant, subjecting the body to the soul, the
senses to reason, in spirit uniting himself to God, he strove to
approach him while remaining bound to his neighbour by the
cords of a wise compassion. In the presence of this man who
trod underfoot carnal pleasures and pierced the stony hearts
of sinners, the whole body of heretics were afraid and the
saints made joyous. He grew at once in age and in grace, experienced an ineffable delight in the salvation of souls, devoted himself entirely to God's Word, and by its means awoke
many thousands to life. Made a preacher and leader to the
people of God, he, unaided by man, created the new preaching order and strengthened it unceasingly by evident and
authentic miracles, for in addition to his deeds of holiness
and his wonderfully beautiful character, that made his life
here so resplendent and so famous, even after death he has
given back health to the sick, speech to the dumb, sight to
the blind, hearing to the deaf, strength to the paralysed—a
sure sign of the more perfect beauty of the soul within. Bound
to us by ties of friendship, before we were raised to the Pontificate, his life carried with it in our eyes certain proofs of
heroic holiness, so that the miracles of which others have
brought us due and solemn witnesses do but confirm what
even without them was established. Hence it is that we are
convinced as also are our people that through his prayers God
may do us mercy and that one who was our friend on earth
will still in heaven hold us in no less affection; wherefore by
the advice of our brothers in the episcopate and of all the
prelates of our Court, we have determined to add his name to
the number of the saints, and do hereby order and command
you on August 5, the eve, that is, of the day when, laying
down his broken earthly body and rich in grace he entered
into the glory of all the saints, to celebrate his feast and to
cause it to be celebrated with full solemnity to the end that
God, in answer to the prayers of one whose life was here an

endless service, may give us grace on earth and in heaven a vision of his glory."

The long-past dream of his mother had come true; her child had set the world ablaze; for since that day of Canonisation, the memory of his name has never been forgotten, but treasured with happy remembrance. It is true that in ages of ignorance, such as followed the eclipse of the Renaissance by the reform, Dominic has stood in the fables of popular history as a fierce and narrow character, for whom thumb-screws and faggots were the only arguments acceptable. But such ignorance has been confined only to a small portion of Christendom. Elsewhere he has stood for truth and freedom. To him have come in Catholic places just those who most truly loved the glorious freedom of the sons of God.

The devotion to him of Savonarola might well have perplexed those who had thought of the Spaniard as a dark and narrow bigot while they hailed the Florentine as the master of freedom, a wide-minded and zealous gospeller. Precisely as a master of freedom it was that Savonarola turned to Dominic and saluted him as the father of the free. Fair Pico della Mirandola, Sir Thomas More's perfect hero, beautiful in face and mind and soul, wrestling in nine hundred theses to solve the pent-up problems of the world, turns, as did Angelo Poliziano the humanist, to the Dominican habit for burial, seeing in its black and white *Beau Seant* the panoply of tolerance and truth. Las Casas, fearless champion of the oppressed, took refuge among the sons of St Dominic, when he found they were at one with him in denouncing the slavery introduced by the Spaniards among the Indians of Mexico. Failing in old age and losing the heart of courage, he sought for its rejuvenation to steadfastness in the ranks of the Preaching Friars.

And of Lacordaire, who is ignorant of the reason of his choice of the Dominicans as his means of re-establishing the faith in the modern world? The eloquence that remains, almost now a legend in Europe, itself indeed pointed to a preaching Order as the one for which he was most fitted; and his love of bodily austerity and the generous impulse that made him so ardent an admirer of physical suffering wrought through love, both further directed him to a monastic life which united in its essential ideal the discipline of fasting and abstinence, of silence, of the sacred psalmody with the free and travelled office of preaching. But, above all, the great motive force that had driven him out of his narrow atheism and made him throw in his lot with Christianity as the universal religion of humanity was his burning belief in freedom as the determining element in character and as the basis of religious faith; it was this love of liberty that particularly moved him to choose the Order of St Dominic as his vocation: "St Dominic had burdened the body but let the will go free . . . had given to his government the form of a monarchy, though tempered by election for superiors and by a parliament for legislation." "If we are asked," said he, in his *Memoir for the Re-establishment in France of the Friars Preachers,* "why we have chosen the Order of Preachers in preference to any other, we reply because it best suits our character, our temper of mind, our aim: our character by its form of government, our temper of mind by its teaching, our aim by its instruments of good, which are chiefly preaching and sacred science. We may perhaps be asked furthermore why we have preferred reviving an ancient Order to founding a new one; we reply—for two reasons, *first* because the grace of being a founder of an Order is the highest and rarest God grants to his saints and one which we have not received; *secondly,* even were God to give us the power of creating a religious Order, we feel sure that after much reflection we could find nothing newer, nothing better adapted to our own time and our own wants than the rule of St Dominic. It has nothing ancient about it but its history, and we do not see for the life of us any need of straining our ingenuity for the simple pleasure of dating only from yesterday." Again he repeats the same view in another place, in his *Life of St Dominic:* "Experience has proved the wisdom of this mode of government. By its means the Order of Friars Preachers has freely accomplished its end, equally free both from license and from oppression. It has managed to combine a genuine respect for authority with a really frank and natural expression of feeling, which reveals from the first the true Christian set free from fear by love. Most religious Orders have undergone reforms which have broken them up into different branches, but that of the Friars Preachers has existed for seven centuries without losing its unity. It has spread throughout the world, nor suffered the separation of one single reformed portion."

Another view of the same characteristic of St Dominic's foundation is put by one of Lacordaire's earliest disciples in a passage of striking contrasts. It occurs in a letter of Requedat, written from the Dominican priory of the Minerva in Rome: "As for me, I am profiting by my abode here under the shadow of the cloister to travel that long road which always remains to be traversed by those who, having once left the Church, return to her by a side-track; I mean the path that leads us back to the Church as little children. I am gradually learning no longer to mistake the cause for its effects, nor the effects for their cause; no longer to accept religious teaching because it happens to coincide with social teaching, but rather to accept that social faith which I can deduce from my religious faith; no longer to love Jesus Christ because I love the poor, but rather to love the poor for the sake of Jesus Christ." And it is for this very reason that he too turned to St Dominic to be trained in his apostolate, to find the imperishable principles on which to rear the fabric of freedom; there as a child of the revolution he could learn the true meaning of freedom, brotherhood, and the equal law. It is the perpetual miracle of Dominic ever to have captured the eager hearts and alert minds of each young school of freedom. Over against the background of his own age (whence date such political institutions as remain to show the freedom of mediæval civilisation), against its restless constitution-making, its reforming vigour, its national spirit, its new temper of art, architecture, music, colour, song, rises the figure of the Spaniard. His slim form shows lightly against the moving pageant of his days, his clear voice rings, his fine eyes gleam, his slender hands are restless in their gesture, his mind and will are in perfect harmony, watching, pausing, then leaping to decision. There is playfulness in his character, yet austerity; he is quick yet even-tempered; in him burns very brightly the full flame of energy and life. Rapid, indomitable, he yet knew the secret of consulting his fellows and trusting them, even weighing in due measure their judgement against his own. It was this that saved him from himself.

Had he followed, as in his early days around Toulouse, his own vehement judgement, he would have remained as full of zeal as ever, but have grown narrower in outlook as the years passed him by. But he had learnt from Peter and Paul the true democracy of Christendom, had seen in the life of his Master the true tale of Christian brotherhood, had learnt (as his old friend Pope Gregory insisted) the true law of freedom in human service. "Because I believe therefore have I spoken" is the epitaph that must be written over his life; because he believed in God, he spoke of God; because he believed in man, he spoke to man.

He believed in his fellows and their power to goodness and remains

> A *swinging wicket*
> *set between*
> *The Unseen and the Seen.*

APPENDIX

The materials used in this life have been chiefly: *The Acts of the Process of Canonisation* recorded in the *Acta Sanctorum* of the Bollandists under August 4 (dated 1233); the *Life of St Dominic*, by Jordan of Saxony, in the same collection (written before 1234); the *Life* by Theodoric of Apoldia, a German Dominican, about the year 1288, also to be found in the *Acta Sanctorum*; and especially the primitive life by Peter Ferrand, O.P., published in the *Analecta Ord. Praed.*, vol. iv, p. 296, the original whence even Jordan of Saxony drew much of his material and the very phrases in which he described his friend. There is an excellent account of this life in the *Analecta Bollandiana*, 1911. Finally, reference has frequently been made to the *History of St Dominic* by Frances Raphael Drane (1891), the *St Dominic* of Jean Guiraud (1901); *Pèlerinages Dominicains*, by Kirsch et Roman (1920); *San Domenico di Guzman* by Barbieri (1922); and *The Inquisition*, by Hoffman Nickerson (1923). A great debt of gratitude is due from the author to Sister Mary Hyacinth Graham, O.P., of St Dominic's Priory, Carisbrooke, to whose patient and laborious kindness he owes more than he can say.

NOTES

CHAPTER I

[1] *Chronicha Ord. Præd.*, p. 6.

[2] Book II, p. 67.

[3] Humbert de Romans, *Vita Sti Dominici*, chap. iii.

[4] The symbolism of later ages saw in this a play upon the name of his followers, *Domini canes*, "the hounds of the Lord," but the earlier writers and artists do not seem to have realised the pun. *Vide* Mandonnet, O.P., "Note de Symbolique mediævale: Domini canes," *Revue de Fribourg*, October, 1912.

[5] Humbert de Romans, chap. iv; and Jordan of Saxony, *Acta SS.*, Aug. 4, p. 545, who refers it, however, to the mother of the saint.

[6] *Analecta Ord. Præd.*, vol. iv, pp. 297–8.

[7] Humbert de Romans, chaps. iii and v.

[8] Jordan of Saxony, *Opera*, pp. 3 and 4.

[9] *Universities of the Middle Ages*, vol. i, p. 472.

[10] Jordan of Saxony tells us that the boy gave up the arts for theology when he considered he had "wasted sufficient time over them." "Sufficient of these straitened years" is the actual phrase (p. 4).

[11] *Acta SS.*, p. 637; *cf.* Jordan, pp. 5 and 6.

[12] *Analecta*, vol. iv, p. 299.

[13] *Acta SS.*, p. 637, and Jordan of Saxony, p. 5.

[14] *Ibid.*, p. 542.

[15] *Mamachi, Annal.*, vol. i, p. 119.

[16] Though his little house is still shown the pilgrims (*Pélerinages Dominicains*, p. 64, 1920).

[17] *Analecta*, vol. iv, p. 299.

[18] Jordan of Saxony speaks of him (*Acta SS.*, p. 543) as still subprior even later when he was in France; the primitive life speaks of him as already subprior when he was in Palencia (*Analecta*, pp. 300 and 301); Stephen of Lombardy in his testimony (*Acta SS.*, p. 637) speaks of him as "Prior or Subprior," but Mamachi reads "Prior or Superior," App. 75, Test. vii.

Owing to a fire in 1505 the archives of the Cathedral of Osma were destroyed; the only contemporary document that remains is the *Escritina de Concordia* of 1201 between the Cathedral Church of Osma and the monastery of St Dominic of Silos. It is reproduced in the third volume of the *Historia del Obispado de Osma* by Lopeárrez, with the signature of *Dominicus Supprior*.

[19] *Acta SS.*, p. 543.

CHAPTER II

[1] *Acta SS.*, p. 544.

[2] Guiraud, *L'Albigeisme Languedocien aux XIIe et XIIIe Siècle.*

[3] *Cf.* Douais, *Les Albigeois, leurs origines*, Paris, 1879. L. Tanon, *Histoire des Tribunaux de l'Inquisition en France*, 1893. Douais, *Documents de l'Inquisition*, etc., Paris, 1900.

[4] *Cartulaire*, i, pp. 148–9.

[5] O'Leary, *Life and Times of St Dominic* (London, 1912), p. 45, and also St Bernard's *Letters*, 241.

[6] *Acta SS.*, p. 544.

[7] *Ibid.*, p. 544.

[8] *Ibid.*, p. 634.

[9] *Ibid.*, p. 641.

[10] *Ibid.*, p. 642.

[11] *Ibid.*

[12] *Ibid.*

[13] *Ibid.*, p. 639.

[14] It was recommended to the Bishops of Christendom by Innocent III in no less than fourteen letters between 1208 and 1212. In Catalonia in 1233 it is found under the jurisdiction of the Dominican Provincial of Spain, but it died out before the second half of the thirteenth century.

[15] *Annales*, London, 1845, p. 182.

[16] *Chronicon*, n. 3, and *Vitæ Fratrum*, p. 322.

[17] Reichert, *Acta Cap. Gen.*, vol. i, p. 81.

[18] *Cartulaire*, i, pp. 243–256 and 415.

CHAPTER III

[1] Guiraud, *St Dominic*, p. 56.

[2] *Analecta*, vol. iv, p. 302.

[3] Douais, *Documents*, etc.

[4] *Acta SS.*, p. 643; *cf.* Humbert de Romans, chap. xliv.

[5] *Cartulaire de St Dominique* (Paris, 1893, vol. i, p. 139).

[6] *Ibid.*, i, p. 148, etc.

[7] *Ibid.*, p. 303.

[8] *Analecta*, vol. iv, p. 302.

[9] *Acta SS.*, p. 401.

[10] *Ibid.*, p. 544.

[11] *Bullarium* O.P., i, p. 1; Mamachi, *Annales*, i, App. 39; *Cartulaire*, i, pp. 277–337.

[12] *Acta SS.*, p. 546.

[13] *Cf.* Gen. Cap. of Rome, 1644: "We declare that at Prouille there is not only the monastery of Nuns of the Order, but also a Priory of Friars Preachers founded by our blessed father, St Dominic, who was himself its Prior, which Priory has been confirmed by Pontifical Bulls" (Reichert, vol. xii, p. 198, M.O.P.).

[14] *Acta SS.*, p. 402.

[15] Chap. xliv.

[16] Douais, *Documents*, etc.

[17] *Cartulaire*, ii, p. 159.

[18] Mamachi, *Annales*, vol. i, p. 250, etc.; *Thierry of Apolda*, chap. viii, n. 95; *Acta SS.*, p. 578 and following.

[19] Mamachi, *Annales*, p. 1, n. 13. *Cartulaire*, ii, pp. 425–453.

[20] LL., f. 248; *cf. Cartulaire*, iii, pp. 78–80.

CHAPTER IV

[1] He is buried in the Cathedral of Osma in the Chapel of the Miraculous Christ under a simple inscription: HIC JACET ILLUSTR. D. DIDACUS ACEVES. EP. OXOMENSIS.

[2] *Analecta*, vol. iv, p. 305.

[3] Costantino d'Orvieto, *Vita Sti Dominici*, nn. 12 and 44; Galvano Flamma, p. 3.

[4] *Analecta*, vol. iv, p. 303.

[5] Thierry of Apolda, *Vita Sti Dominici*, chap. ii, n. 35.

[6] *Acta SS.*, p. 552.

[7] *Cartulaire*, i, pp. 480–483.

[8] "From the date that the Crusade began to the death of Earl de Montfort, the Blessed Dominic *remained* an unceasing preacher of the Divine Word" (Jordan of Saxony, p. 12).

[9] St Thomas (*Sent.* iv, qu. 2, art. 3, ad 5): "The Church does not persecute men in order to induce them through violence to believe, but to prevent them corrupting others and lest so great a sin remain unpunished."

[10] "In 1535, so savage were the persecutions, that Pope Paul III, with that gentleness which almost invariably has characterised the Popes of Rome in dealing with heresy, wrote to Francis protesting against the horrible and execrable punishments inflicted on the Lutherans, and warned him that although he acted from good motives, yet he must remember that God the Creator, when in this world, used mercy rather than rigorous justice, and that it was a cruel death to burn a man alive; he therefore prayed and required the King [Francis I of France] to appease the fury and rigour of his justice and adopt a policy of mercy and pardon. This noble protest was effective, and some clemency was afterwards shown" (*The Story of Paris*, by Thomas Okey, p. 169. London, 1906).

[11] Galvano Flamma, p. 3.

[12] *Cartulaire*, i, p. 450.

[13] *Ibid.*, i, pp. 515–6; iii, p. 270. April 17, 1221.

[14] *Acta SS.*, p. 546.

[15] We learn from Bishop Foulques (Balme, p. 515) that already the friars had taken a vow of poverty.

[16] *Cartulaire*, i, p. 526.

[17] Labbe, *Concilia*, t. xi, part i, p. 131.

[18] *Analecta*, vol. iv, p. 306.

[19] *Ibid.*, p. 306.

[20] *Codex Ruten.*, p. 79. This manuscript is preserved in the archives of the Order in Rome.

[21] Echard and Quetif, *Scriptores Ord. Prœd.*, t. i, p. 16.

[22] Humbert, *Echard*, i, p. 28.

[23] *Analecta*, vol. iv, p. 306. Jordan of Saxony, pp. 14–15.

[24] *Cartulaire*, ii, p. 58, etc.

[25] *Acta SS.*, p. 634.

[26] *Bullarium Ord. Prœd.*, vol. i, p. 2.

[27] *Cartulaire*, ii, p. 71.

[28] *Bullar. Ord.*, i, p. 4, and *Cartulaire*, ii, p. 86.

[29] *Cartulaire*, i, p. 243.

[30] Quetif and Echard, i, p. 9 n.

[31] Jordan of Saxony, p. 14.

[32] *Bullarium*, p. 5, and *Cartulaire*, ii, pp. 91–2.

[33] *Acta SS.*, p. 546.

[34] *Cf.* the deposition of William of Montferrat in the Process of Canonisation, p. 631.

[35] "Ou non valsenhe agols val bagols," *Cartulaire*, i, p. 169.

[36] *Acta SS.*, p. 546; *Analecta*, pp. 306–7.

[37] Humbert de Romans, *Vita*, n. 26, and Jordan of Saxony, p. 15.

[38] This list gives exactly sixteen, and is possibly a truer census than that of Bernard Guy.

[39] Feb. 11, 1218; *Cartulaire*, ii, pp. 156–7.

[40] Deposition of John in the *Process. Acta SS.*, p. 634.

[41] *Vitæ Fratrum*, p. 328, and *Cartulaire*, ii, pp. 142–3.

[42] *Chronica Conventus Bononiensis* (Rome, 1903), p. 3; Galvano Flamma, p. 13.

[43] *Analecta*, vol. iv, p. 307, and Jordan of Saxony, p. 16.

CHAPTER V

[1] Cantu, in his *Storia Universale*, vol. vi, p. 87 n. (Turin, 1887), has shown from a Cambridge MS. that the name Waldenses existed before the birth of Valdez.

[2] *De articulis fidei et sacramentis ecclesiæ*; cf. Denifle, O.P., *Archiv für Litteratur und Kirchengeschichte des Mittelalters*, i, p. 419; the Bull is to be found in Tiraboschi, *Vetera Humiliatorum monumenta*, 1766–68, Milan, vol. ii, p. 139.

[3] For a more full rendering of the details of this mission career in the South of France consult the charming volume by C. M. Antony: *In St Dominic's Country* (Longmans, 1912).

[4] *Cartulaire*, i, pp. 511–12 n.

[5] John of Navarre in *Process of Canonisation. Acta SS.*, p. 634.

[6] *Ibid.*

[7] *Ibid.*, p. 576.

[8] *Opera*, p. 18.

[9] *Chronica Convent. Bonon.*, p. 3; Jordan of Saxony, p. 13; Thierry of Apolda, chap. vii, n. 8.

[10] *Acta SS.*, p. 574.

[11] He spent long nights in the Catacombs, *Vitæ Fratrum*, p. 84.

[12] Thierry of Apolda, chap. vii, n. 80.

[13] *Acta SS.*, p. 538.

[14] *Cartulaire*, ii, pp. 306–7.

[15] Jordan of Saxony, p. 19; Humbert de Romans, n. 28; *Vitæ Fratrum*, pp. 70–1.

[16] Bernard Guy, *Primorum Beati Dominici Sociorum . . . elogia*, chap. vii.

[17] *Vitæ Fratrum*, p. 74; *Cartulaire*, ii, p. 285.

[18] Jordan of Saxony, p. 19.

[19] *Ibid.*, p. 2.

[20] *Acta SS.*, p. 547.

[21] *Vitæ Fratrum*, p. 72; Galvano Flamma, p. 20; *Cartulaire*, ii, pp. 339–344.

[22] In the *Parva Legenda* of Francisco Pipino, O.P., 1322 (*Anal. Ord. Præd.*, 1921, p. 197), we are told that the Order was confirmed by Pope Honorius III in 1216, and "the third year after he confirmed also its constitutions."

[23] Deposition of William of Montferrat. *Acta SS.*, p. 631.

[24] *Chron. Conven. Bon.*, p. 39; Galvano Flamma, p. 23.

[25] *Cartulaire*, iii, pp. 48–9.

[26] Deposition of Stephen, n. 4. *Acta SS.*, p. 638.

[27] *Acta SS.*, p. 634; *Chron. Conven. Bon.*, pp. 37–8.

[28] *Ibid.*, Aug., vol. iii, p. 312, etc.

[29] *Contra Impugnantes Dei cultum, Opera*, t. 29, p. 29.

[30] *Vitæ Fratrum*, p. 138.

[31] *Annales*, p. 644.

[32] *Opera Omnia*, ii, p. 41, Ed. Berthier, Paris, 1888.

CHAPTER VI

[1] Is this the knife with its yellow boxwood handle and its rusty unpointed blade which is shown so proudly to the pilgrim by the Theresiani Paolini in the Via Palazuolo in Florence?

[2] *Chron. Conven. Bon.*, p. 38; Galvano Flamma, p. 29.

[3] *Cf. Il.*, vii, *Centenario di San Domenico*, anno ii, fasc. iii, and Encyclical of Benedict XV, *Fausto appetente die*, June 29, 1921.

CHAPTER VII

[1] *Cf. Analecta Ord. Præd.*, 1896, p. 622.

[2] It is characteristic of the spirit of the new Order to find this laid down in the earliest official commentary on the Constitutions: "So zealously must the studies be pursued that in their interests the sterner obligations of the Order are to be dispensed, not only lest the studies should fail, but even lest they should suffer." Humbert, *Opera*, vol. ii, p. 26 (1263).

[3] Oxford, 1913.

CHAPTER VIII

[1] *Vitæ Fratrum*, p. 41.

[2] *Ibid.*, p. 74.

[3] It is interesting to note how large a portion of the primitive life (pp. 307–309) is devoted to the account of Reginald, his cure and his character.

[4] *Cf.* Humbert de Romans, *Vita*, n. 27.

[5] *Opera*, p. 18.

[6] Gilbert, the first English Provincial, was so gained, *Cartulaire*, ii, p. 184.

[7] *Vitæ Fratrum*, p. 170.

[8] *Ibid.*, pp. 26, 128.

[9] *Ibid.*, p. 20.

[10] Jordan of Saxony, pp. 19, 20.

[11] *Cf. Acta SS.*, p. 548.

[12] *Cf.* Jordan of Saxony, pp. 20–23.

CHAPTER IX

[1] Mamachi, *Annales*, Appendix.

[2] *Acta SS.*, p. 595.

[3] In this chapter a general reference should here be made to the *Process of Canonisation*, *Acta SS.*, pp. 628–643.

[4] *Cf.* Humbert de Romans, n. 28.

[5] B. Cæcilia, *Miracula B. Dominici*, n. 10.

[6] *Chron. Conven. Bon.*, pp. 36–37.

[7] *Ibid.*, p. 37.

[8] *Acta SS.*, p. 636; Rudolph of Faenza in *Process*, n. 3.

[9] *Ibid.*, p. 634.

[10] *Ibid.*, p. 573; Humbert, n. 26.

[11] *Chron. Conven. Bon.*, p. 38; *Analecta*, t. 2, pp. 644–645.

[12] *Ibid.*, p. 44.

[13] Galvano Flamma, p. 29.

CHAPTER X

[1] *Cartulaire*, iii, pp. 140–145.

[2] *Cf. Acta SS.*, pp. 557 and 604, and Humbert de Romans, n. 21.

[3] *Vitæ Fratrum*, p. 325; Galvano Flamma, p. 36; *Chron. Conven. Bon.*, p. 54.

[4] Bernard Guy, *Codex Rutensis*, p. 82.

[5] *Analecta*, vol. iv, p. 314.

[6] Galvano Flamma, p. 37; *Chron. Conven. Bon.*, p. 56.

[7] *Acta SS.*, p. 599.

[8] *Analecta*, vol. iv, p. 317.

[9] The whole of the monument can be studied in detail in the sumptuous volume by Père Berthier, O.P., *Le Tombeau de St Dominique à Bologne* (Paris, 1895), where photogravures of delicacy and finish reproduce something of the refinement and distinction of the various artists.